THE NEW WE

Politics is a childish game

THE NEW WE

Politics is a childish game

Stacy McKay

Emerald Crown Press

www.EmeraldCrownPress.com

Published by Emerald Crown Press
www.EmeraldCrownPress.com

For information about special discounts for bulk purchases, please contact Emerald Crown Press at info@emeraldcrownpress.com

For information on booking Stacy McKay for speaking engagements, please visit www.stacymckay.com

ISBN

Hardcover: 978-1-966747-01-7
Paperback: 978-1-966747-00-0
Digital: 978-1-966747-02-4
Library of Congress Control Number: 2025926414

Printed in the United States of America

To my emerald boys — the gems of my life.

DEAR READER

Have you ever felt like you had to pick a side — just because everyone else was? Maybe it was in school, on a team, or even in your own group chat. Let's be honest — sometimes "picking a side" happens faster than we even realize, and suddenly we're wondering who started the argument in the first place.

It's easy to believe that one side is right, and the other is wrong. But here's the trap: once we start labeling people as *us* and *them,* we stop seeing classmates, teammates, family, and friends, and start seeing opponents, rivals, enemies, or villains in a story we didn't even mean to write. That's when hurtful things start to happen.

This book isn't about proving one side right and the other wrong. It's about showing what can happen when invisible lines — between ideas, beliefs, or even best friends — start to feel like walls.

At the heart of this story are Sammy and Cleo, two best friends who suddenly find themselves on opposite sides of a culture war at school. Sammy feels betrayed when Cleo joins a group that challenges everything he stands for. Cleo feels torn between her loyalty and her new allegiances. They both think they're doing the right thing...and neither one finds that comforting.

You might find yourself siding with one character and then switching to the other halfway through. That's okay. Everyone in this story has a reason for what they do. They all see the world through their own lens (some more clearly than others).

Nobody here has the whole picture. Just like me. Just like you.

If you catch yourself thinking one character is "good" and another is "bad," that's human too. But remember — people are never just one thing. Even the kindest hearts make mistakes, and even the people we disagree with have stories worth listening to. Every character in this book believes they're doing the right thing.

Sometimes they are right. Sometimes they're hilariously, heartbreakingly wrong.

I'm not here to take sides. I'm here to hold up a mirror to us as a society — to show what happens when we let labels decide who we are. And I'm here to inspire young people to do what you always do best — make a better world than the one you came into.

The danger isn't in disagreeing. It's in letting disagreement decide who we care about, who we listen to, and who we see as worthy.

It's tempting to want simple answers, because simple feels safe. But simple doesn't mean true. We're messy, complicated, beautiful humans — full of contradictions, grace, and surprises.

This story doesn't hand out easy answers (because life rarely does either). But it does remind us how much we need each other, even when we don't see eye to eye.

If we hold onto that truth, it will lead us back — again and again — to what matters most: friendship, respect, and the courage to understand. And most importantly, the strength to stand together, even when the world tells us not to.

SAMMY

"Where's my wristlet?!" Sammy manically rummaged around the messy backseat of his father's Tesla, the only electric car within 100 miles of Emerald, his rural Pennsylvania town. He turned frantically to his colorful tie-dye backpack, his manicured hands shuffling things around with growing panic. "And my soccer cleats! Nothing is ever where I need it! I can't *live* like this!"

Many call him Pepper, because of how *very spicy* his attitude can be. But probably his most fitting nickname is the one his family calls him: "Lleno" (pronounced "yay-no"), the Spanish word for "full." This name originated when his parents first met him at two months old, the gorgeous and joyous brown-eyed and black-haired infant that would make them a family, as a tiny baby in Colombia. This nickname was given to best capture his essence which is...full. Full of energy, full of passion, full of confidence, full of feminine energy, full of masculine bravado, full of *life!*

"Moooommm! I need those cleats!" Sammy bellowed towards the house, as he hurriedly and inefficiently sprinted in circles, shouting and mumbling curse words under his breath.

"I found them," his mom Mac yelled out the upstairs bedroom window. "I fell on my duff when I tripped over them. They were shoved under the rug in your dumpster of a room!"

Sammy remembered now that he had been hiding them there, along with many other items including clothing, art supplies, and board games. His rug was his best friend when it came to the chore of cleaning up. He shoved items under the rug until it looked like a sad lumpy heap resembling his hippie parents' compost pile outside.

His mom cracked the second-story window and tossed the shoes out. The first one hit the ground.

A rustled thud into the bushes below.

The second shoe fell to the ground with a...*ba-gawwwwk!* Out from the bushes ran Sprinkles, one of the family's tiny pet bantam chickens. She puffed up her body and shook her little black and white feathers, dust and grass flying everywhere. Sammy ran over to make sure she was okay. She darted behind the barn, disgusted at the disturbance to her morning nap.

"Poor Sprinkles! Mom you *beast*!" he shouted jokingly, while rummaging through the garden for his cleats.

"She's fine! And besides, that chicken would be nuggets right now if we hadn't saved her from the meat farm. A shoe won't kill her." She smirked and blew Sammy a kiss through the window screen.

He grabbed the shoes and hopped back into the car, laughing under his breath at his mom's salty attitude. He loved her cranky and humorous way of talking, as she made nearly everything funny in her own permanently annoyed sort of way.

He continued rummaging around desperately looking for his wristlet. To have a day without it would be...unimaginable. Impossible. Torture.

He slumped down into the car, starting to lose hope, when he glanced at the door. "Here it is! UGH! I can die happy now!" he mumbled to himself. Sammy wiggled the wristlet free from the side compartment of the car door and clutched it to his chest in an embrace, like long lost friends at the Arrivals Hall of the airport.

His wristlet was small and beige, with a wide loop for slipping over his wrist and a gleaming gold "S" embossed on the front — S for Sammy, of course. After months of saving money from his pet sitting gigs around town, he finally worked up the courage to step inside the fanciest store in the shopping center — the one he'd only ever admired from the outside through its ornate windows lined with crystal chandeliers.

Once inside, he beelined straight for the back to the sale rack, the one place where his dream of taking something home had a fighting chance. To both his delight and disbelief, the math worked out — barely — but enough to make the wristlet his.

It became his prized possession: proof that he could make things happen, that he belonged anywhere he wanted to be. He was so proud of buying it himself that he treated it like a tiny miracle — his "baby," as he called it.

Sammy slipped it on his wrist and Vogue-posed for no one in particular.

He then got back up and stood next to the car, scanning down his outfit to ensure he looked as show-stopping as possible before heading to school.

He wore a red T-shirt that read *"I've Been Good-Ish All Year,"* and although it was September, he was totally unconcerned with its misplaced holiday theme. Coupled with this were his favorite black running tights, which had orange flames climbing up the legs from the ankles to the knees. He finished the ensemble with white sneakers that had iridescent rainbow stripes down both sides which changed color based on the lighting. When he had first seen these at the store, he declared they were perfect, because his favorite color is, of course, "rainbow."

All the colors. Not just one.

Lleno.

"Pep, you're going to love today's soundtrack!" Sammy's dad Alex said enthusiastically, sitting down in the driver's seat and closing the door.

Oh no, Sammy thought, rushing to get in the car just as it started to drizzle. *Let me guess, today we'll have to figure out the meaning of life in the 8-minute ride to school.*

Sammy's dad was an intellectual and loved to listen to educational programs in the mornings, usually about the weightiest of topics — the science of the cosmos, or collective consciousness, or comparative analyses of various religions. As points were made, he paused the audio and excitedly talked to Sammy about these hefty lessons.

He hit "play" to resume the program as he began to drive. *"...and so today, we will share the inspiring, amazing story of Harriet Tubman and the seismic accomplishments that one human being can achieve."*

Alex started clapping. "I *told* you it was good!"

Sammy perked up. Social causes were very important to him, especially those around equality, and he was a particular fan of Harriet, having even done a book report on her in second grade. Back then, when other 7-year-old students were doing reports on animals or Santa Claus, Sammy chose Harriet Tubman, to his elementary teacher's delight and amazement.

While he was very familiar with this story, he was never tired of hearing it again and again, daydreaming about how he could have an impact like that on the world.

But only if he could do it without breaking a nail.

Beep, beep! the car horn squawked. Sammy startled from a daydream to realize they had already arrived at Cleo's house. She wasn't outside which annoyed him, even though he never would have waited outside in the rain for her. With an eye roll, he begrudgingly snatched the umbrella his dad offered him and stomped to the front door, intentionally overemphasizing his struggle to open it in case she was watching.

Inside Cleo's house, things were just as hectic. "Sammy's here! Why isn't your lunch packed?" asked Cleo's father, Reginald. He spoke in a low bass voice that ricocheted effortlessly throughout the house, a voice which came in quite handy when he gave his Sunday sermons.

Reginald's shaved, dark head nearly grazed the tops of the door frames as he passed through the house briskly, dressed to perfection in a blue suit with a lovely green and blue paisley tie, and perfectly polished tan shoes. He wore shimmering gold cufflinks, which Sammy had admired before, as he was a lover of eye-catching fashion. He had never seen such opulent attire worn by a man before. After all, Sammy's dad Alex's version of dressing up is wearing sneakers instead of sandals.

Sammy could hear Reginald from inside as he walked up the path to their house. "I need to get going too! Prayer group starts in less than half an hour."

Sammy noticed Reginald peeking out the front window as he approached. Reginald's eyes scanned his attire from toe to head, from the pink projecting off the iridescent stripes of his shoes, to bright orange flames crawling up his leggings, to the wallet dangling from his wrist.

It lasted only a split second — something someone else who was unaccustomed to being judged on the daily might not have noticed — but Sammy could practically feel Reginald's eyes on him and hear the grumble of his disapproving thoughts.

Because he liked Reginald, he would let it slide. This time. After all, old-fashioned viewpoints could be hard to break.

Before Sammy had even taken a full step onto the porch, Reginald gave a quick shake of his head like he was knocking the thoughts out, then forced a smile and exchanged waves through the window with Alex who was waiting in the car.

"Ready!" sang Cleo, darling in both appearances and demeanor. She wore a plaid blue and white dress with a white ruffled collar, and a red bow at her neck. Her hair was full of curly black ringlets that went in all directions, but most stunningly they grazed across her eyebrows right above her sea-green eyes.

Cleo was one of the only people who truly accepted Sammy's label-breaking eccentricities. He capital L-O-V-E-S himself (glitter toss), but maybe a tiny part of him would have preferred that other kids understood him too.

Not that he cared, though. As if.

Sammy knew that at times, Cleo felt like an outsider too. She was a Black girl in a predominantly white rural area, so it made sense that she understood how it felt to stand out. Like Sammy and his outfits — immediately drawing attention when he entered a room, instantly being assessed and noticed by all. He and Cleo had always shared this similar reality and felt each other's unspoken challenges without having to say a word.

She scooped up her pink backpack and yellow raincoat, stepped on a chair and gave her father a kiss on the cheek, dropped back down with a thud as her white Converse shoes hit the floor, and ran out the door.

"It's about time!" Sammy snarked. "Here, use my umbrella. I know how you hate it when your hair gets wet." He handed her his treasured Colombian flag umbrella. He got it at the World Soccer Classic when his family took him and Cleo on a trip to Miami to attend the event. As an all-star soccer player and a huge fan of the sport, attending the event was a bucket list item for Sammy.

In addition to the vibrant red, yellow, and blue of the umbrella, Sammy had recently wrapped silver glitter tape up and down the handle for a little more flair.

"Oh my gosh, *Sammy*!! This is so over the top! When did you do this?" she said with a grin.

"Rain can't dampen my fashion, okay?" Sammy pursed his lips and popped his hip to add to the show. Cleo giggled.

They both huddled under the umbrella as they walked to the car, while Cleo untangled pieces of the loose glitter tape from her hair.

"Sorry I'm a little late!" she said. "I was making flyers for Benjamin's new club. I had so much homework last night that I had to get up early this morning to get them done in time."

Sammy didn't think much of Benjamin Rosa. Many times, he felt that Benjamin bullied him for his "non-masculine" ways. On the other hand, Cleo and Benjamin were not exactly *friends,* but they were *friendly*. They went to the same church and spent a lot of time together in the after-school youth group there.

Sammy didn't like the sound of this. Why was Cleo working on a new club with Benjamin? Sammy resented how Benjamin used poor Cleo like a pawn and took advantage of her sweet nature to manipulate her. Plus, if she was going to be doing free work for someone, Sammy figured it might as well be for him instead!

Cleo and Sammy both hopped in the backseat of the car, a habit that they had gotten into as young kids carpooling together. Because they were such close friends, neither of them had ever wanted to change things and move to the front seat when they became old enough. No one spoke about it, it just never happened.

Sammy intentionally slammed the door to wake his dad from his podcast trance. Alex scolded him for the slam and then greeted Cleo with a silent smile and a wave, not wanting to interrupt their conversation.

"Mmm-hmm…" Sammy sassed. "What club is this? That dope always has to be at the center of something. Did he start a new church? Are you Benjamin's first worshipper?" he chuckled.

Cleo ignored the jab. "I told you about this! He's starting a new club at school. We aren't sure what it will be called yet, but the point of it is to talk to students about what they want to improve at school, and Benjamin says he will fix it!"

Sammy sneered. "That makes no sense. He can't fix a thing. What kind of control do we kids have at school? Basically none! Tell him that I propose that every student gets a million dollars from the school! Can he do that? Pfft!" he scoffed condescendingly.

"Come on Sammy, be reasonable. Benjamin said that he could help us raise money for new gym equipment, get us more choices of food in the cafeteria, help start an after-school prayer group, and he even wants to cut out a class in the middle of the day to give us time for club jobs!" she said.

"That is ABSURD! You'll believe anything! You and I both know that he can't do those things. He is just saying that to get you to follow him." Sammy was getting more irritated by the moment.

"You remember when Benjamin's family donated enough money to *single-handedly* save my dad's church when he almost had to close it last year? I've seen how the Rosas can make things happen — and Benjamin is no different! My dad thinks this is a great idea too and asked me to help Benjamin since we owe him and his family so much."

Sammy began to ponder the situation. He knew the kind of guy that Benjamin was, and he couldn't believe that this club was about helping people. Sammy was obsessed with figuring out what Benjamin was getting out of starting a club. He assumed it was just to flash his money and power around.

The tiff came to a halt, and Cleo and Sammy both stared out the window in silence as the narrator continued with Tubman's tale on the radio. After what seemed like a silent eternity, their car came to a stop in front of the school. Alex reached his right arm around and grabbed the back of the passenger seat and twisted around.

"Here we are! Sammy, be sure to bring all your extra clothes home from your locker tonight, your mom wants to do a wash. I don't want to have to drive you back to the school tonight to get them!"

"Yeah, yeah, yeah" Sammy said.

"Goodbye, love you!" Alex leaned back and gave Sammy a grazed kiss across the cheek as he scooted across the back seat and out the passenger side door after Cleo.

"Bye dad, you creeper," snipped Sammy. He and Cleo scurried out the door and up the stairs to the school.

"You should come to the club meeting today! Benjamin says everyone is invited," Cleo said as she pulled open the school door. "Just remember two things. One, it costs $5 to join. And two..." she hesitated and glanced at Sammy's legs, "um, he told me in the past that he hates those flame pants of yours, so you may want to change into your gym shorts or something before the club meeting."

Record screech.

This cut like a knife. Sammy's safest harbor, his closest friend, the one person who wouldn't judge him. He was in disbelief. Had he just heard her say this? Was she just passing on a hurtful note from a moronic dope, or did she really accept a stance like this?

He dashed after her, knowing she was trying to drop that bomb and run away unscathed.

"Excuuuuse me?!" Sammy exclaimed, ready to launch into his alpha-attack mode. "First of all, that meathead discussed my pants with you? Then again, of course, I can see how he is the boss of fashion with his wrinkled soccer jersey and sweatpants look. How is that not on every runway? I am not taking fashion advice from some mimbo like him!"

Sammy's lack of respect for Benjamin internally validated his own clothing choices to himself more than ever. He felt emboldened.

For a moment.

Cleo didn't immediately join in the scolding of Benjamin's comments, which hurt Sammy. He knew he could be like a quick-heat teapot, already boiling after just seconds, and maybe he should have cooled down and just let the issue drop.

Nah. What fun was that?

"Would you accept it if Benjamin told you to straighten your hair to look 'whiter' like him? Or talk in a lower voice so you sound more like a man because he thinks guys are better? Who is he to tell us to change who we are to be like him? How dare he!" Sammy was fuming.

"Of course, that would be horrible, and I would never do it. But this isn't a race or gender thing," Cleo said, shutting down the point that Sammy was stumbling to make.

"But it *is* basically the same thing! He is trying to make me change to fit his alpha-jock rules."

"They are just pants, Sammy."

True, pants aren't race or gender. But they were so much more to Sammy than pants. They were part of his identity. His freedom of expression. His "right to be me."

He couldn't tell if she truly didn't understand his stance, or if Benjamin had influenced her in some way. Sammy's questions seemed almost anticipated by her, and she offered back what felt like emotionless, rehearsed responses.

He stopped at his locker as Cleo continued to hers, just 20 or so lockers down the hall. He continued, shouting down the hall. "And you are PAYING this guy? For what?"

"It is the club fee," she said. "He said he will use the money for running the club."

"What does that mean?" Sammy pushed back.

"He said that our money will help him make the school better. I know from church that donating money is the best way to help the less fortunate, and for people to come together to support those who need it most. I'm not sure what he is using it for yet, but I'm sure it will be good." She walked back to Sammy's locker to escort him to homeroom.

"This is a public school. We don't pay anything to go here. What money is he going to save us?" Sammy asked.

Cleo paused. "You just wait and see. Don't you want to be in this club?"

"What are the 'club jobs' that he's talking about?" Sammy pestered, aimed more at tripping up Cleo and ultimately Benjamin, than out of actual curiosity for the answer.

"Just COME!" she said, walking briskly away into their shared homeroom.

Ms. Traben poked her head out of the door as the bell rang. "Sammy! Let's go! I don't want to have to mark you as late!"

Sammy slammed the locker door and hurried into class. He scanned the room as he walked to his desk, and his gaze immediately locked on to Benjamin.

No surprise there — a rumpled old red soccer T-shirt and gray sweatpants.

Sammy laughed at a banded indentation that encircled Benjamin's unkempt red hair the entire way around his head, left from his ever-present baseball cap.

Sammy remembered Benjamin's dislike of his flame pants, so he backed out of the aisle he had started to walk down and headed down the next aisle, closer to Benjamin so he couldn't miss it, hoping to provoke an interaction. Benjamin's glare at Sammy's flames was obvious. In exchange, Sammy looked at Benjamin's wrinkled gray sweatpants, let out a theatrically judgmental giggle, covered his mouth condescendingly and sat down.

Throughout homeroom and the first two class periods that day, Sammy stewed with anger. He couldn't understand how Cleo could be tricked into this nonsense — or how Benjamin could think he would get away with it. Taking people's money for nothing? It was outrageous. Who did he think he was?

Sammy's curiosity, judgment, and annoyance had twisted together into something electric. Instead of brushing off the situation, he found himself plotting. He could show up to that meeting, watch every move, and figure out exactly what Benjamin was planning. Maybe he would give a speech and purposely torpedo the club, or better yet, slip in as the model recruit, snag one of those ridiculous "club jobs," and quietly wreck the whole operation from the inside. Taking the club down would be the perfect way to make sure no one ever tried to mess with his best friend again.

He paused, considering the possibilities. If the job paid, maybe he could finally buy the sewing machine he'd been wanting so he could bring his fashion designs to life.

Then he caught himself. He was getting swept up in the wrong way. He would get a club job to destroy the club. Period. That would teach Benjamin Rosa.

And if it helped him sew his masterpieces, all the better.

BACK ON TRACK

The first meeting of Benjamin's yet-to-be-named club began during recess "promptly at 1pm" according to Cleo's flyers. The last thing that Sammy wanted to do during his only free time of the day was to listen to Benjamin's rants and raves. Sammy usually used recess to catch up on the latest EHS gossip, or work on his tan by soaking up a few rays.

Since transferring here, Benjamin always reminded everyone that they should be thankful for having recess at all, because city kids like him didn't get recess in junior high or high school. Sammy glanced down and admired his sun-kissed skin.

Thank God I'm a country boy.

He paused, gagging on his words. *Did I just think that?*

As a self-proclaimed city boy (who just *happened* to have lived his entire life in the country) he decided to ratchet up his plan to move to Paris the day after graduation…before whoever just spoke in his head changed his mind.

Sammy sat at lunch clinging to a copy of Cleo's meticulously hand-scrawled flyer, on which she had used every colored pencil she owned to create a beautifully colorful image.

He had to admit that the rainbow was pretty. However, he was positive that she did that to hurt him, because rainbow was his favorite color. There was simply no other explanation.

Sammy scanned down the flyer further, trying to decipher what the club was about. It encouraged everyone to join Benjamin and Cleo at recess to learn about a new club that was going to improve the lives of EHS students. His eyes stopped at one jarring phrase.

Help us, help you!
Together we will fix the school and get things
BACK ON TRACK!

Next to that phrase, he noticed a black blob with what looked like two hairy spider legs coming out of the top. He squinted his eyes. What *was* that? Cleo had never been much of an artist, certainly nowhere near as good as Sammy. But he conceded it wasn't fair to compare. After all he was going to be in museums someday.

Cleo dropped her tray on the table. "Hey Pepper! Do you like my flyer? Pretty cool, huh?" she said pridefully.

"I'm not in the mood," Sammy grunted. "But since you asked, what is this black blob? Did you draw Benjamin, the killer black widow spider?"

Sammy dramatically turned the paper sideways and upside down, showing great struggle to decipher the image.

"Female spiders do that, not male ones. And anyway, it's not a spider, that is a train back on the tracks! Benjamin Rosa is going to get the school BACK ON TRACK!"

"I didn't know it was off track," piped in Ronald, another student at the lunch table. Sammy smiled, thrilled at having an ally in this fight.

Ronald Ross was neither a close friend, nor a foe of Sammy or Cleo. More than anything, they were perpetually annoyed at how he refused to take a side during Sammy and Cleo's all-too-frequent tiffs during lunch. Ronald had strong convictions, but they rarely favored

Sammy or Cleo exclusively. He often suggested compromise, but neither of them was interested in that type of senseless concession.

"Well, it *is* off track!" Cleo implored, proud that she knew this tidbit of intel before so many others. "We are off-track, and Benjamin will be the one to get us BACK ON TRACK!"

"Why do you keep parroting that stupid phrase?" Sammy said.

"It's not stupid, Pepper! You're just jealous you didn't think of doing this!" Cleo said. She immediately regretted the outburst, knowing that Sammy's defensiveness would take this spat to a whole new level.

"I didn't think of stealing other kids' money, THAT'S true! I would *never* think of that!" Sammy said indignantly. He began to see that his grip on his bestie was weakening. He had to act fast.

He decided to make her pick between them.

"Go be with your *boyfriend* Benjamin, but you can count me out."

"He's not my boyfriend!" Cleo said dismissively. "It is your choice, but I'll be there either way if you change your mind."

Well, that backfired.

"Wait, Sam, before you go." Ronald paused. "Why don't you go to their club meeting? At least listen to what they say and maybe you can find something you like about it. I'm going to go and see what this is all about. Come with me!"

Torn between his curiosity and disgust, Sammy decided to do what he does best — leave the audience wanting more.

"I bet you'd like that!" he said. "I'll do whatever I feel like doing, you'll just have to wait and see." With that, he stormed away from the table and out of the lunchroom.

Although his mind was subconsciously made up to attend, Sammy went through the motions of debate as he stood directionless in the hallway.

Now what? If I go, I'd be feeding the massive ego of that Bozo-min Rosa.

He paused with pride. *That's a great name, why haven't I thought of that before? Maybe I'll try that out at the meeting.* "Great meeting Bozomin! I've decided I'll pay you $5...to shut up and get out of my life!"

He was getting more and more pleased at the idea of attending and stealing the limelight with his zingers.

He paused, realizing that he had accidentally decided to go. He knew that people expected him to be there, and he had to admit that even he didn't hate Benjamin enough to allow an event to happen without Sammy there. How miserably boring!

So, it was decided. Sammy was attending the club meeting during recess. Because he had stormed out of the lunchroom 15 minutes early, he now had to figure out something to do to pass the time until recess started.

He couldn't go back and admit he had nowhere to go or nothing to do. That would take all the panache out of his dramatic exit. Sammy had to come up with a distraction. He knew he had a lot of anger to burn off before the meeting. Then he got an idea.

He tip-toe-ran down the hallway and gently leaned against the gym door, testing if it was locked. To his delight it was open, and miraculously, the gym was abandoned. He kicked off his rainbow shoes, whose stripes were undeniably blue now. He ran over to the blue mats, pushed one to the floor, raised his hands, pointed his toe, and launched into one of his competitive gymnastics team's floor exercise routines from last year's competition at the Naval Academy. Much like that day, he gave a gold-medal-winning performance.

Cartwheel, then a round-off, then three back handsprings, then a mat run into another cartwheel, somersault, one leg leap, twist...he paused. He started to feel beads of sweat coming down his forehead.

He knew he couldn't show up dripping and running like bad mascara. He had to stop quickly before he looked like he just got out of the pool. Thankfully, his goal was accomplished, and he felt much better.

Sammy had gotten good over the years of knowing when he needed to burn off some energy and frustration before he lashed out. Just like his dog Athena when she goes un-walked, if he didn't find a way to burn off his energy, Sammy could act up. He had never gone so far as to chew on his dad's slippers, but you couldn't put anything past him if he was angry enough.

He pushed the blue mat back up against the wall, slipped back into his rainbow sneakers, dabbed the sweat from his forehead, and headed down the hall to the recess door.

Get ready Bozomin, Sammy's ready to tumble.

THE SIZZLE

As he walked into the sunshine, Sammy saw a cluster of kids standing by the flagpole. Looming tallest above all other heads was a red mop top of hair stuffed messily into a baseball cap.

Benjamin.

Next to him Cleo was standing with a clipboard in front of a line of kids who seemed to be signing their names onto a piece of paper clipped onto it. Sammy zoned in on that clipboard, trying to figure out where it came from. Could Ms. Traben be enabling this by lending him that? Bozomin has everyone fooled!

Sammy stood there for a minute, doing one last reconsideration of his choice to attend. But the temptation to go was just too over-whelming. He began to cross the playground. Cleo saw him and gave him a big wave. Several kids looked over at him to see what she was so excited about.

This was a happy accident — at least now he could make a grand entrance.

Benjamin glanced over too. He saw Sammy's flame pants again and rolled his eyes.

Sammy knew — from what the other kids said and from the look on Benjamin's face whenever he walked into the room — that Benjamin found him annoying, confusing, and far too attention-seeking with his rule-bending ways. Sammy was equally confused about Benjamin — how could anyone embrace sports and video games as a complete lifestyle?

Guess they would have to agree to disagree.

"Come sign-up here, Sammy!" Cleo beckoned.

"No thanks," snipped Sammy. "I don't want to be on any list. I'm just here to listen." He turned around and realized he was the last in line. He could tell that the meeting was about to begin by how Benjamin had taken off his hat and was attempting to tame his hair into a presentable pile upon his head.

"Hello everyone! I'd like to thank you all for being here today for the first meeting of the BOT club. We are going to do some great things here at…"

"What's the BOT club?" Sammy barked. "I didn't know this had a name."

"I was going to get to that, but yes, we are calling this the BOT club, named after what we plan to do — get things BACK ON TRACK!" He smiled with pride at his very clever motto.

Not AGAIN! Sammy thought. He now knew why Cleo kept repeating that stupid phrase. He resisted his temptation to make a snippy remark and instead just rolled his eyes and the speech continued.

"Now, this is going to be the day that your lives change forever! We, the BOTs, stand for honesty! Teamwork! Improvement! We want to get the school BACK ON TRACK!"

Benjamin started to pace around, making eye contact with the attendees. "Let's be honest, things have gotten out of control here, and we need to restore some order at Emerald High School."

He paused, seeming to await applause or accolades of some kind. He was met with silence.

This was clearly not what he had anticipated. Benjamin seemed to be improvising, stumbling to give substantive examples to support his claims. "Like…all the junky decorations people have on their lockers. These are a mess! Magnets and streamers and photos and balloons…they make the school look ridiculous. This isn't kindergarten! We don't need to know every feeling you have or every celebrity crush! Keep the decorations inside the lockers."

Sammy was fuming. The outside of his locker was a carefully curated scrapbook of friend photos, and glitter, and sports, and celebrities, and artwork, all conveying parts of his unique personality.

He couldn't believe Benjamin was trying to take away their freedom of speech. As far as Sammy was concerned, people should be able to express themselves however they want without exception! His heart was racing.

On second thought, he did agree that no one should be caught dead with streamers or tacky balloons on their locker. Benjamin was clearly referring to Kevin Pfeiffer with that remark. An exception should probably be made to force Kevin take those down. They were tragic.

"If you say we shouldn't have to know about every feeling people have, aren't you forcing your feelings of dislike of the decorations on others?" Sammy's head snapped to the left and he saw Ronald standing there, speaking confidently.

"I *feel* that the decorations…er…I mean I *think* that they reflect poorly on all of us. We need unity!" Benjamin looked proud in his handling of the question.

"But that doesn't make sense, either everyone gets to express their opinions, or no one does. You can't silence others." Ronald continued calmly.

"Or our clothing!" Benjamin continued, ignoring Ronald's existence. "Before I moved here, I attended a private school in the city, and we had uniforms. They were fantastic! We never had to think about what to wear or waste our brain power on worrying about fashion or picking out outfits. Everyone looked the same — respectable, nice, and neat. I don't like walking down the hallway and seeing people in short shorts, or pants with flamesss..." he stumbled over his words, catching Sammy's knowing glare.

"The point is, we need to have order. Aren't you tired of the chaos around here? We need to get this school under control and back on track. Now I know that I probably can't get the school to require uniforms, but I will try! My dad is on the school board and will help us pull strings to get what we want. Either way, we as students can start to get things back on track *right now*!"

Benjamin motioned to Cleo who brought over a dry erase board that Sammy was sure was from Ms. Traben's classroom too.

Benjamin drew a number one on the board, and then the word ORDER. "There are a lot of things that I want us to do together this year, but we need to start with getting things in order. We need to take action. My first order of business will be to ensure that every member of the BOT club takes down not only their locker decorations, but everyone else's too. If you see decorations in the hallway, you should politely ask the locker's owner to take them down. If, in 24 hours they have not, then you should gently remove them, fold them, and give them to the locker's owner. This is our school, and we need to take it back. They will thank us for getting the school BACK ON TRACK!"

Sammy was appalled. The idea of anyone taking down his decorations felt like an attack on everything he believed in. Who did Benjamin think he was, acting like uniformity was some kind of rule? To Sammy, the whole "everyone-must-be-the-same" campaign was ridiculous. Being unique wasn't a problem to fix — it was the best part of living.

Benjamin continued by writing a number two on the board, and then the word UNIFORM. "Now as I said, it may take me a little while to get the school to agree to uniforms. But don't worry, I'm sure I can get it done. For now, though, the BOTs are going to get it started. From now on, all members of the BOTs will wear plain dark pants, blue or black, and a shirt that is red, orange, or pink... well, pink is only for girls *obviously*!" he chuckled.

Sammy fumed, looking down at his own shoes which were reflecting pink at that moment.

"This is the club started by me, Benjamin Rosa, so only rosy colors for us! Remember, red, orange, or pink. No frilly prints, or scarves, or ridiculous accessories. We will all look unified, and people will see us and know that we are a team — like in sports! Then they will want to join us. Won't that be great?!"

Sammy glanced down at his red Christmas shirt. Of all days to wear red. Ugh. He wanted to split it at the neck and rip it open down his chest, swirl it around his head like a lasso, and throw it off in a theatrical move of defiance. After a moment of pondering, he concluded that running around all day shirtless seemed only *slightly* worse than being identified with the BOTs.

Sammy's intense gaze was burning a hole through Cleo, who was obviously trying to avoid eye contact with Sammy as she stood silently next to Benjamin. Sammy was perplexed. Why was she going along with this? Is her dad making her do this? What is this hold that Benjamin has on her?

Undeniably, Cleo and Benjamin's friendship was strictly platonic. Cleo had never dated anyone before, and Sammy couldn't imagine her first relationship being with someone like Benjamin. They just didn't fit that way — Cleo was thoughtful, quiet, and steady, while Benjamin was all big gestures and spotlight energy. Whatever they were to each other, it definitely wasn't romantic.

Benjamin had tried to venture outside of his "all-looks-no-substance type" once when he dated Indigo Ortiz, a brilliant and strong Latina classmate with the heart of an activist, and a deep passion for making the world a better place. Their relationship didn't end well. It didn't take Indigo long to realize that Benjamin was more concerned with his outward appearance and reputation than he was in tackling the issues that matter to her in the world. So, she broke his heart and hit the bricks.

"Number three!" Benjamin's handwriting was getting worse as he continued to scrawl on the board. He clearly had not planned for how much space he would be using on the board, as he was already needing to squeeze sentences in margins and hyphenate simple words onto the next line.

"JOBS. I am excited to tell you about these! Here at the school, we can't wait around for people to take care of things for us...no way! There are *so* many things wrong here, and to get us back on track, we as the BOTs need to pitch in and come up with solutions to the problems ourselves. We can't wait for the school to solve things for us!"

"What are these jobs? Will we get paid for them?" Ronald questioned.

Benjamin smiled. "Well, it depends."

"Depends on what?" Sammy spouted.

"Depends on *you*," Benjamin said. "We will have a few jobs that I'll make up, and those jobs will be paid with the club dues money. I'm still working on that..." Sammy could tell from the distant look in Benjamin's eyes that he had not developed any jobs, or even any sort of plan for that yet.

He was seeing a pattern. Benjamin's plan was to get people to buy into something he hadn't even created yet. Sammy had heard his mom say something like this before, talking about a car salesman. *"He's not selling the steak; he's selling the sizzle!"*

As Sammy glanced around at the smiles on so many kids' smiling faces, he realized that Benjamin is good at this. As confusing as that was — since Sammy thought Benjamin was perpetually floundering and unfocused — it seemed that, to a lot of kids, he was speaking their language. He was selling that sizzle.

But what, *really*, is he selling?

24

Benjamin continued. "Only the best of the best students will get one of MY jobs. But don't worry, there's still hope for the rest of you!"

Sammy marveled at how oblivious Benjamin was to how condescending he sounded.

"YOU can create jobs!" Benjamin was emphatic now. "You don't need to wait for jobs to be created by me. You can create your own jobs now! See something that needs to be fixed around the school? You can fix it! Get your idea approved by me and go for it. I can't do this alone — it will take an army of us to get this place under control again."

Surprisingly, this sounded interesting to Sammy. Almost instantly, an idea came to his mind. He was always frustrated at how there are no vegetarian options in the lunchroom. Maybe he could bring in some of his dad's famous vegetarian chili and sell it! He felt a smile wash across his face which he quickly ushered away, for fear that Benjamin would see it and feel validation that he may have presented a good idea.

"It could be anything. You can help us get back on track and make some money for yourself in the process! Now, we want these jobs to all be part of the BOT movement, and we as the club need your help too! Because of this, you will need to give the BOT club $1 for every $5 you make. This way, we can use this money to continue to spread our message and create a better school for everyone. It will be your way to give back to this club that will give so much to you." Benjamin had been talking with such enthusiasm that he was nearly out of breath.

The bell rang, marking the end of recess. "One more thing, speaking of money. We will be having another BOT meeting next week, same time, same place, here at recess. Please come with your $5 club entry fee. Feel free to bring kids who are the *type* of people that you think will fit into our club. Also come with more ideas on how we can get the school BACK ON TRACK!"

As he was finishing his sentence, he and Cleo began rushing to gather up the flyers, dry erase markers and board, sign-up sheets, clipboards, and other odds and ends, signaling an end to the meeting.

"Why would we need to give you 20% of the money that we make ourselves? We earned it, not you!" Sammy exclaimed righteously, ignoring Benjamin's attempted mic drop.

Ronald piped in too. "He has a point. If we make the money, we should be able to keep it. For those that want to contribute to the BOTs, they should of course be able to. But it shouldn't be forced. If you and the BOTs are doing a good job, you will get donations. And anyway, the goal isn't to make money, right? It is to get the school back on track, as you say."

Ronald awaited a response calmly.

Benjamin stood up from picking up folders and papers under the bench. For the second time today, he had a look of complete surprise, this time with some disgust peppered in, as things were going "off track" from what he had planned.

The irony.

"If there truly is someone who wants to keep all the money for themselves and doesn't want to give back to the club that has given so much to them, then we wouldn't consider them a friend of the BOTs anyway. Those people have no allegiance or honor, and that would be a shame!" He smirked. "Hypothetically, of course."

"What exactly have the BOTs given to us..." Sammy was cut off by the sound of Miss Markusic calling the end of recess.

Benjamin and Cleo rushed to gather up the remaining items, haphazardly tossing things into two cardboard boxes. "Look guys, I don't know what to tell you. Either you are with us, or you aren't. I'm not begging." And with that, Benjamin walked off, strutting away with empty hands.

Cleo sheepishly smiled at Sammy as she dashed away alone, her slight frame struggling to carry the overflowing boxes. Sammy followed behind in disgust, silently picking up the items that Cleo unknowingly dropped in her struggles.

Together, yet alone. He hoped this wasn't their permanent new arrangement.

The New "We"

Three days had passed since Benjamin's first meeting of the BOTs. Sammy and Cleo had awkwardly avoided talking much about it since then. They each had rightfully assumed that their views were so contrasting on the topic, that nothing good would come from debating it. Eventually, they may need to discuss it with one another, but for now, they both seemed satisfied with ignoring it altogether.

This morning, Sammy was outside in the rain — grumbling and complaining as he waited for Reginald and Cleo to pick him up. He was standing in front of his house, and while there was a roof overhang, it was above the second story of the house which did Sammy nearly no good when it came to rain protection, especially when the wind was blowing in sideways.

The winding driveway of his family's old farmhouse was very long, so when the weather was nice on the days it was his turn to be picked up, Sammy would make the trek up the driveway and wait at the street for Cleo and Reginald. But, as a rule of life, Sammy refused to interact with anything or anyone that was distasteful to him, and that included weather patterns.

In these cases, Reginald would drive his beautiful black sedan down the gravel driveway, kicking up dust and mud as he rounded each turn to pick Sammy up at the door. The perfectly waxed and glimmering surface of his black car showed every ounce of mud and dirt that the driveway had tattooed upon it. Sammy loved watching the fancy car bumping down the lane, partly because he admired the class and elegance of the Arco family vehicle — Sammy adored Reginald's style in general — and partly because he found it so funny how ill-placed a car that classy seemed against the backdrop of the neighbor cows doing their carefree munching and fertilizing in the rainy field.

Today was no exception. Down the way the beautiful car came, except Sammy was too cranky to admire it this morning. He was annoyed at having to wait in the rain for even a minute, even though Cleo and her dad were five minutes early.

The car came to a stop. Sammy ran across the cobblestone walkway and under the grapevine covered archway, opening the door and dashing into the car.

"It's really coming down out there!" Reginald said.

"You can say that again!" Sammy said with a bite, wanting sympathy again for his rain struggles. He turned to smirk at Cleo. She grinned back, rolling her eyes at Sammy's dramatic ways.

"That is quite a coat you have there, Sammy!" Reginald motioned toward his raincoat, which was black with metallic silver lightning bolts on the front of it. In the center of the back of the coat was an umbrella with different colored raindrops falling around it. However, this part of the jacket was pressed against the back of the seat, so Reginald truly didn't know *how* fantastic the coat was…yet.

Sammy saw right through the veiled judgment. Seeing no point in trying to change his mind, he decided to match Reginald's faux excitement.

"THANKS!" he exclaimed. "All the boys have one!" He chuckled at the preposterous nature of that thought.

Imagine Bozomin in this coat! He'd never pull something like this off! He wishes.

Sammy suddenly became aware of Cleo's not-so-subtle attempt to hide something under her raincoat. It was a short drive to school, and inexplicably she had taken the jacket off and laid it on top of a lumpy pile of items on her lap.

"What's going on there?" Sammy said, motioning to her lap.

"Oh nothing," she said.

Sammy knew there was no way Cleo could ever believe such an answer would satisfy him, but he couldn't blame her for trying. He pursed his lips and gave her a side eye glance.

"Okay, okay, these are just some things for a BOT event today, no big deal" she said sheepishly.

Sammy's first reaction was dismay. He didn't know anything about a BOT event! Was she intentionally hiding it from him? He pondered if he should ask her why she didn't tell him, or act as if he didn't care. After almost no debate, he opted for the former.

"I didn't know there was an event today. Am I banned?"

"You didn't sign up on the list, so we assumed you weren't interested," she said quickly.

Cleo using the word "we" referring to her and Benjamin and not referring to Sammy and Cleo (the only "we" she ever used to care about) burned him up.

She had a new "we."

"You're right, I'm *not* interested," Sammy said dismissively. His restraint lasted about five seconds, until curiosity won out. "What stupid event is it, anyway?"

"It isn't your type of thing. If you want, I can invite you to future BOT events that I think you'd enjoy!" It was clear that she was trying to smooth things over in as vague a way as possible and get out of this car with peace still intact.

Cleo's eyes darted toward the window. The school was in sight. She began to gather up the items in the hidden bundle under her jacket, all the while keeping her gaze focused on her escape route into the school. It was obvious to Sammy that she wanted to get out of there before he could ask anything else.

"You can drop us off here, Dad!" she urgently exclaimed.

"What? Don't be silly, I'm not dropping you off in the middle of traffic! We're almost there," Reginald huffed.

Sammy was watching all of this suspiciously. He couldn't figure out what was going on with her.

The car pulled into the student drop off roundabout and stopped next to the Pickup/Dropoff sign. "Have a good day, kids!" Reginald bellowed.

"Bye, Dad," Cleo said breathlessly, and dashed out of the car.

"What's with her?" Reginald asked, twisting back to look at Sammy.

"That's what I'd like to know." Sammy took his time in grabbing his backpack, zipping up his raincoat, and throwing up his hood. "Thanks, Mr. A."

The rain was really coming down now. Sammy remembered that Reginald had not seen the back of his jacket yet. He got out of the car, ever so slowly, flipped up his hood, and sauntered up the walkway into the school. Sammy knew Reginald made a habit of watching to make sure that the kids got in the building before leaving, so he was positive that he'd see the colorful display on the back.

His heart was full at the thought. He smiled to himself, and just as he walked in the building, Sammy looked over his left shoulder and waved to him. Reginald smiled and gave a half wave, just before doing a quick roll of his eyes as he drove away.

"Sammy!" He turned around to see Ms. Traben rushing after him. Sammy *adored* his teacher Ms. Traben. As she ran her blonde, curly hair bounced in her eyes. From the moment she had become Sammy's teacher, Miss Traben had been a safe place of comfort for him when he wasn't at home. She saw through his tough candy-coated exterior to the sensitive little nut inside, and she was committed to doing everything she could to nurture that part of him.

"So, are you going to join Benjamin Rosa's club?" She smiled, having no idea the landmine she had stepped on.

Sammy was fuming now. "Benjamin Rosa's club?" If he hadn't made his mind up about it before, this conversation sure would have put a nail in the coffin.

He choked back his disgust. "I don't think so, no."

Her face fell. "Oh no, why not? It sounds like a great idea! I love seeing kids get involved in causes. Benjamin is such a passionate kid, and it is great to see him getting active in something he believes in!"

Sammy's frustration started to bubble and boil as he looked at her naïve smile.

"He is passionate, I'll give him that," Sammy said with disdain. "But it's not the kind of club I'm interested in joining."

"Why not? He told me he is trying to help support us as the leaders of the school with strong leadership from the students too, which I think is great! I have been helping him by giving the BOTs basic supplies and what not, as I know how expensive things can get." She smiled with pride.

There it was. Sammy *knew* she was supporting the BOTs. He was vindicated and annoyed all at the same time. She obviously couldn't see what Benjamin was really about.

Sammy paused, considering if he should impose on her a lifelong exile from his life. The punishment should fit the crime, and she chose to support Benjamin. What crime could be worse?

Then again, he couldn't imagine how much suffering she would experience by not enjoying his delightful company daily.

He decided that this would be cruel and unusual punishment. He'd give her the benefit of the doubt…this time.

He knew he wasn't going to change her mind in these five minutes before class started, so he fought against all his urges and took the high road.

Gasp. He was getting soft.

"Okay, I'll think about it. See you in class!" He walked away with as big of a smile as he could paint over the natural disgust that was tattooed on his face.

He knew (from how many times Cleo had told him) that his forced grin looked more like he had gas than anything else. But it seemed to have worked, as Ms. Traben's face was illuminated with a proud smile, having assessed this as an inspiring teacher/student moment.

Sammy continued down the hall, trying to avoid eye contact with anyone else for fear of being lassoed into another conversation about Benjamin. When he arrived near his locker, he looked down the hallway and saw that Cleo was not at hers. The two of them knew each other's schedules by heart, and Sammy saw that as very odd. He walked up to a locker and reached up to input the combination, and he stopped.

Wow I must be out of it today! This isn't my locker! He went a few lockers down and then stopped again. *What am I doing? 626 is....* he paused. He looked back and saw that he had been at the right locker the first time.

Something was different.

Suddenly, his blood ran cold. Where was the Picasso-like self-portrait that Sammy had sketched of himself? Where was the poster of his favorite musical group Theo and Gwen? Where was his magnet-framed Vogue magazine cover featuring Harry Styles in a dress? Where was his Real Madrid soccer flag? Where was Sammy's favorite photo of him and Cleo from last year's Halloween ball? The door of his locker was completely...and utterly...bare.

He glanced down the hallway. Most of the lockers were now bare. Lockers that previously had been a rainbow of exhibited art, and notes on dry erase boards, and magnets, and photos…now an ocean of the hideous gray-ish/green-ish color that seems only to exist to paint lockers.

He looked over at Kevin Pfeiffer's locker and was in disbelief. He saw Cleo standing there, now wearing her elusive raincoat. She was meticulously but quickly taking down Kevin's collages and hideous 3D giraffes that he had stuck to the door. They were there to signal to everyone that Kevin planned to be a zookeeper, a fact that he repeated endlessly.

She glanced guiltily both ways in the hallway. While she had been seen by many students, luckily none of them had been Kevin. Sammy noticed now that she had a box of garbage bags and was neatly folding and placing Kevin's locker items into one.

He immediately realized that those bags must have been one of the things that she was hiding under her coat in the car. He was incensed.

A few lockers down, Sammy saw Benjamin with another garbage bag, tearing down artwork and photos in bedazzled frames from the outside of Terri Anderson's locker. He was much less meticulous than Cleo and instead was ripping down Terri's decorations and crinkling them into a garbage bag, without so much as a thought for her things, or her feelings.

Sammy was in absolute disbelief. Things seemed to be moving in slow motion. He opened his locker and noticed a large black garbage bag that had been placed inside. None of this made sense — how did the BOTs get inside his locker? How did they get into *everyone's* lockers? He sat there, staring at the bag, trying to piece everything together.

Then, the lightbulb went off. He realized he had never changed his locker combination.

At the start of the school year, the maintenance department set dummy locker combinations for every locker, which were the same as the locker numbers themselves. Sammy's locker, 626, still had the combination of 626. It didn't exactly take rocket science intelligence from the BOTs to crack those codes.

Sammy remembered being told a million times to change the combination to secure his stuff after that first day. He now regretted that he never did. As he gazed back and forth down the hall, by the looks of it, nobody else had heeded that advice either.

They had assumed they were safe among friends. Clearly, they weren't.

He opened the garbage bag, looked inside, and was gobsmacked. Inside, he found his Harry Styles Vogue cover, and the self-portrait, and the Theo and Gwen cut-out, and the soccer flag, and the photo of he and Cleo, all folded neatly in a pile inside. His heart dropped into his stomach.

That perfect pile stopped him in his tracks.

It was clearly Cleo's meticulous work.

She was the one who'd taken down his decorations.

He paused, tears forming in his eyes, both from the loss of beauty on the front of his locker, as well as the outright betrayal. For the second time this week, he was speechless. He looked over at her and their eyes met through his tears. For a minute, she paused and offered an apologetic look. Sammy's tears turned to rage.

He noticed her red shirt and black pants, the exact same colors that Benjamin had on as he defaced Terri's locker. Sammy remembered back to Cleo's red shirt yesterday too. He'd been blinded by his love of Cleo's cute strawberry shirt to see the signs from the very beginning. And the day before, she'd worn her red glitter shirt that he also adored.

It dawned on him — those had been her BOT uniforms! And now, to add insult to injury, she was carrying out Benjamin's orders to clean off all the lockers against students' wills.

Sammy could get past a few monochromatic shirt choices, but this...this utter abuse of privacy and respect...he didn't see how he could forgive this.

One truth hit him like a safe. Cleo was officially one of them. She was a BOT!

Still locked in eye contact with her, Sammy's tears turned to rage, and he slammed the locker which sent a deafening echo down the hallway. All hallway noise ceased as students turned to see what was going on. Benjamin looked over at Sammy with a smirk as he continued haphazardly tearing and ripping off the remainder of items from Terri's locker, unphased.

Sammy pointed at Benjamin and shouted, "you won't get away with this! How *dare* you take away our decorations?!" He couldn't stop himself. "We have the right to express ourselves any way we want to! I will do *whatever it takes* to stop you from trying to take over this school. You can't control us!"

Suddenly, while still looking at Benjamin, Sammy heard singular clapping coming from a student down the hall. Benjamin noticed too, and as he looked over, his smirk dropped into a look of confused sadness. Sammy turned around and saw that the clapper was Indigo Ortiz, the ex-girlfriend that broke Benjamin's heart.

Indigo stood there, in a long and flowy bohemian navy dress, with mini gold metallic stars adorning it. She had more than a dozen bracelets on each wrist, at least four rings on each hand, and her hair was tied back in a braid with feathers woven into it. She was the epitome of self-expression and unapologetic confidence, just like Sammy was.

She let out a yelp of approval. "You can say that again, Sammy!"

She walked up next to him and, facing Benjamin whose entire body was now frozen with confusion, she looked him straight in the eye. "I don't know where you get off thinking this is right or okay, but there are a lot of us who like to express ourselves." She gestured to Sammy's shoes — looking magenta right now — then down to her own outfit. "We won't apologize for being different. Different from you, different from each other. This school doesn't need uniforms and clean lockers and students spending all their time doing jobs for you! What we really need is more tolerance and caring for one another…we need LOVE!"

Sammy was thrilled to have an ally in this battle. However, as he looked at the bohemian sprite next to him, he began to see things a bit more clearly. What if Benjamin was doing all of this *because* of Indigo? What if he was trying to control everyone because he couldn't control her?

Sammy knew Benjamin didn't accept rejection easily. His litany of school-centric issues didn't seem to truly be what was at the center of the motives here. In some ways, that made Sammy feel better, to realize that this monumental change in Cleo was likely spurned by something as silly as her accomplice's teenage broken heart.

This made the moat between them somehow not feel as wide, or as permanent.

While Benjamin clearly wanted to smooth things over with Indigo, he chose to go on the offensive. "Give it a rest, Indy! No one touched your locker, so why are you sticking your nose into this?"

"That is *so* like you Benny!" she said with disgust.

Benny? Sammy chuckled. *I prefer Bozomin.*

"Of course, all you worry about is you and your friends, and 'forget about everyone else,'" she continued. Something doesn't *have* to affect me personally for me to care! I am happy to stand up to selfish bullies like you for what is right!"

Sammy was impressed with how angry Indigo seemed to be in her words, and yet how cool her outward demeanor seemed to be.

Benjamin's face was a mix of anger, confusion, and sadness. Indigo's opinion clearly still mattered to him, but he kept up the alpha-fight.

"We are taking down locker decorations, not stealing lunch money! I am sick of the mess around this school — it seems like no one is in charge. Kids can't be allowed to do anything they want —

they need to be led! I'm going to get this school back on track!" He tried to reclaim his power by turning his clearly hurt facial expression into a forced self-righteous smile.

Sammy couldn't believe any of this. But the hardest part was seeing his best friend Cleo submissively standing by Benjamin's side, and by doing so, supporting what Sammy saw as a personal assault.

Indigo wasn't done with Benjamin yet. "No one needs you to tell them what to do, Benny. Students should be free to do as they please without someone like you forcing your own made-up rules on them. Those decorations weren't hurting anyone! But now you have hurt those students, all because you feel entitled to control areas that aren't yours. We won't stand for this!"

Sammy realized that Indigo's "we" referred at least in part to her and him, which was amusing to him since today was their first time interacting.

Well, if Cleo is part of a new "we," then so am I!

He realized he didn't know Indigo very well, but she did seem to share his views of the world. He wondered if this would be a better way to pick friends going forward. Losing Cleo made him question everything.

"Shame on you!" Indigo sneered at Benjamin. She grabbed Sammy by the elbow and dragged him down the hallway into Miss Corgan's class. She either didn't remember, or didn't care, that Sammy wasn't in her class, or even in her grade. But at that moment, Sammy couldn't be happier to be in exactly the wrong place, with exactly the right person.

CANNON

The next few weeks were a complete disaster. No one was talking to anyone, fights were breaking out between friends, and everyone was taking sides. Some were choosing to align with Indigo, or Benjamin, or Sammy, or Cleo, or even Mr. Compromise: Ronald.

Sammy simply couldn't accept that Ronald wouldn't pick a side already, especially with how serious things had gotten. Ronald was nothing but a big wimp as far as he was concerned. How could he be friends with someone like that?

But at that moment, he didn't have much of a choice. Sammy and Cleo hadn't spoken since the locker cleansing. Try as he might, he simply could not make sense of why she had done this. Cleo was always the one to support Sammy and everything about his uniqueness, and while he had always felt secure in this, he now realized he had taken it for granted.

Without her, Sammy felt unanchored. He felt alone. He felt… vulnerable.

While he had many choices of replacement friends in his grade, the excitement of this activism movement had made returning to snooze-worthy chatter about bad lunches, or how mean Mr. Kadlub is for giving homework over the weekends, seem somehow irrelevant now. Sammy had to align with someone interesting, so for now, middle-of-the-road Roadkill Ronald would have to do.

Ronald tried so hard to keep the peace, but to Sammy, his ideas just seemed so simple and bland. They never seemed to catch on. He had no *flash* or *pizzazz* to his platform, which if you ask Sammy, was the cornerstone of any movement. The majority of classmates would probably admit that Ronald's ideas were logical compromises on paper, but why compromise when you can fight to get *everything* you want? True, by going with the one-extreme-or-the-other model, if your side didn't win, you'd be left with nothing. Still, compromise was boring.

And Sammy was not about to lose to Bozomin.

Sammy reached into his pocket and pulled out a crumpled piece of paper, re-reading a note from Indigo repeatedly to unlock its secret meaning. This morning, he had found it shoved inside of his locker, and it asked him for a meeting at recess. He almost overlooked it — normally it would have been put in the handmade purple felt pocket labeled "Fan Mail" that Sammy had made for the outside of his locker, but that too came down with Cleo's betrayal.

He didn't know exactly why, but since the blow-up a few days ago, he and Indigo had been exchanging little pleasantries in the hall, mocking smiles of Benjamin, and knowing waves like friends just checking in on one another. He couldn't wait to see what this meeting was all about.

But first, he had to get through another excruciating Cleo-less lunch.

Sammy felt helpless, so to gain back power, he was capital-E *Expressing* himself. Today, he wore knee high glittery socks that just skimmed the bottom of his shorts, to complement the EHS team's soccer jersey that he wore on top, the same soccer jersey that Benjamin treasures as a tribute to his masculinity.

Sammy was so pleased at this provocation. Having Benjamin see his precious soccer shirt being worn with a glittery socks — on a boy — tickled him.

Sammy looked across the lunchroom to the Red Sea — a cluster of red, orange and pink shirts in the corner by the windows. This was typically an upperclassmen section of the lunchroom where older students like Benjamin and Indigo would eat, with all the social prestige that came along with it. Sammy and Cleo had always been stuck watching that corner from a distance.

Well, at least, it *used* to be that way.

Now, in that sea of red, Sammy saw Cleo sitting there among the BOTs, looking more confident than he had seen her look in a long time. She glanced at Sammy, their eyes locking momentarily, before she snapped the look away and began laughing with the crowd.

All of this felt like a knife to Sammy's heart. He deeply missed his friend and was both consumed with anger at her for betraying him, and jealousy at not being included in what looked like a very "cool-kid club." But his principles were the most important thing, and he refused to sell out to anyone just for acceptance.

He pulled his glance from the devil-red corner to survey his own table and was unimpressed with the motley crew he was surrounded by. Across from him was Ronald, rambling on about how he thought attendance in class should be optional, because kids should be free to decide how much instruction they needed.

"As long as they pass the tests and assignments, what business was it of the teachers to enforce attendance?" Ronald argued.

To Ronald's right sat Cici Bubber, already mid-rant about how the school had "lost its moral compass." If the lunch table had superlatives, she'd be crowned *Most Likely to Join the BOTs* now that Cleo was gone. A proud country girl with a sharp tongue, Cici never missed a chance to remind people her grandpa fought in the Marines — and that the school considering making the Pledge of Allegiance optional was "basically un-American."

On Ronald's left, Maryam Duale Elmi and Autumn Norman were cracking up over something, and their laughter was contagious as always. Maryam's parents had come to Emerald from Somalia as refugees, and Autumn was adopted from the city by a Jewish family when she was two. They'd been kindred spirits from the day they met, and those two practically glowed compared to everyone else slumped over their pizza slices. Sammy wished he could find a way into their orbit. Those girls had energy he could use.

Just then the bell rang.

Recess.

Sammy was excited, not only because he was pent up with angry energy again and knew he needed to burn it off — his plan was to outshine Benjamin in soccer to cheer himself up — but also because he was meeting with Indigo today. He had no idea what the meeting was about, but he figured it was probably to gossip about something idiotic that Benjamin was doing.

Sammy ran to his locker, dropped off his lunch bag and books, grabbed his wristlet — living up to his motto "always dress to impress" — and headed outside.

Again, he saw the red wash of shirts, this time over by the jungle gym. It didn't look like a meeting was going on, more like the members of the group had decided that they were their only social group now.

"Pepper!" Indigo shouted, waving her bracelet-covered arm at him.

It was strange to hear her use the nickname that only Cleo had ever called him at school. Indigo was incredibly cool and already reaching nickname-status with an older girl like her was a huge win, especially in his goal of upsetting Benjamin. But that name was special to Sammy, and only a few close family members and his former best friend called him that.

"Settle down! You can't rush perfection," he shouted with sass. She belly-laughed, which filled Sammy with glee. He slowed down his walking pace a little, milking the joke a bit more.

Indigo was sitting on the rock wall that bordered the school yard, dividing the school grounds from the quiet residential neighborhood next to it. Sammy jumped up on the wall and flung his wristlet on the wall next to him.

Indigo glanced down at his wristlet and smiled. "Thanks for meeting me here, Sammy. I think we need to talk." Indigo looked earnest and focused on her yet-to-be-named purpose.

"Let's hear it," Sammy said.

"What do you think about Benjamin and his BOTs?" she asked.

"I think it is the stupidest thing on the planet," he blurted. "I have no idea why anyone would be a part of something like that. Giving money for someone to boss you around makes no sense."

"I completely agree. The whole thing is insane to me." She smirked and rolled her eyes.

Sammy tried not to be seen sneaking glances at Cleo in the Red Sea near the flagpole, but he couldn't help himself. His angry curiosity could not be satiated. Indigo put her hand on his shoulder. "I bet it hurts having your best friend leave you for that group."

Sammy shook her hand off. "She didn't leave me, and besides, we weren't great friends anyway," he said emphatically. This was an obvious lie, and he knew that Indigo knew that too, but he also knew she'd never question him.

People rarely did.

"Well either way, I think we need to do something about it," she said.

There it was again, that "we."

Sammy's eyes perked up. Do something about this? *Was* there something they could do? He was energized at the thought but came up empty on what that solution was.

"What do you have in mind?" He leaned in as he said this, feeling a mix of mischievousness, excitement, and vengeance.

Indigo smiled. "Well, there is only one thing I can think of. We need to make our *own* group. We can put these tontos in their place."

"Tontos?"

"Sorry, in Spanish it means idiots. Fools. Bozos."

Perfect name for Bozomin.

She continued. "Besides, I don't want our school to get stricter. I want more freedoms! More love! More friendship! Unlike the BOTs, I want us to help everyone, not just those who think like us."

This all sounded amazing to Sammy.

"You even want to help the BOTs?" he asked.

"Well, they can help themselves," she contradicted, giggling. "Our club will be the club of Goodness, Love, and Opportunity to be ourselves. Because of this, and I'd like our club to be called the GLO club...because we will glow with love for everyone!" she said with a smile.

"Except for the BOTs," Sammy said sassily. They bumped against each other as they laughed heartily at the joke.

"We can figure out the details as we go, but what do you think? Are you in?" Indigo asked eagerly.

He was a bit surprised that she would bring this to him first, as he barely knew her, and being that he was younger than her, that was standardly a status-killer for any high schooler. But like so many, she seemed to truly want Sammy's approval.

He paused, suggesting he was deep in thought. But the truth was, he was only creating a drumroll for his elusive response. After what seemed like an eternity, he rendered his verdict.

"Let's take them down," he said with a mischievous smile.

Indigo beamed.

The cannon had been fired.

A Dimming Glo

A few weeks later, Sammy sat in class staring at Cleo's empty seat. He was angry and sad at the way things had turned out between them. Benjamin's seat was empty too, but that didn't sadden him in the least. Today, Cleo and Benjamin were excused from school because they were at a church retreat together. Sammy imagined Cleo and Benjamin sitting on a rock next to a picturesque and peaceful river in the woods, a setting like every church retreat locale that has ever been, at least as Sammy envisioned it. He imagined them laughing, and plotting, and planning future BOT events.

He was also unable to consider their conversation without imagining that Sammy himself was a central topic. He assumed they were talking about his rainbow shoes, or his wristlet, or how strange it was that he didn't want to break-and-enter into innocent students' lockers and steal their artwork and photographs. Well, let them talk! Because when they got back, they were in for a big surprise.

Sammy and Indigo had spent the last few weeks laying out their plan for the GLOs. They had specifically chosen this day to be their GLO launch — with Benjamin and Cleo away, the BOTs may play!

When the class bell rang, Sammy reached the door just in time to see Indigo outside waiting for him.

"How many BOTs do you think we will convert?" Indigo inquired excitedly.

"Probably most of them," said Sammy with an eye roll. "Why would you want to be a BOT when the GLOs have arrived?"

He planned to get all the non-BOT kids to join, and most of the BOTs too, if he could work his charms. He even planned to get Roadkill Ronald to finally pick a side, a challenge that he figured could be easily overcome with a dose of Sammy Charm.

Sammy opened up his locker and pulled out the remaining personalized handmade invitations that he had handed out to the most popular kids in school, in an effort to create a buzz. He knew that nothing got people more interested in something than if they thought it was exclusive, and that they were uniquely selected to be invited. Also, it couldn't hurt to have the flashiest people in school as part of the GLOs. People love to follow those that they look up to.

On the flip side, he figured that *not* being invited to something like this was even more tempting. So, either way, he knew he was playing the situation perfectly, flattering those he invited, and tempting those he hadn't.

The invitations were clean and classy, as only Sammy would do it. He used white card stock that he found in his mother's office and had diligently cut the pieces into perfect squares. He then used his fanciest art pens, only the most regal of colors — gold and silver of course — to adorn the invitations with his best cursive handwriting.

You are invited to join the newest student club
— the club for regular people just like us,
who want to make the school a better place!
Do you want your life to be filled with
Goodness
Love and
Opportunities *to be yourself?*
*Then the **GLO Club** is for you!*

Below that, Sammy and Indigo had signed their names in cursive, Indigo first in silver, and Sammy in gold.

Obviously.

"I am in love with these invitations! Thank you for making them. This definitely sets us apart from Benjamin and his raggedy clipboard!" Indigo giggled.

For Sammy, praise from an older girl like Indigo, especially one as popular as her and one who hated Benjamin almost as much as he did, made her opinion one of the most important things to him right now.

She had also asked Sammy to put together the handouts for the meeting as well as the agenda. Sammy agreed to everything, because in the heat of the moment he was thrilled to be asked. He also believed greatly in the movement. Additionally, and maybe even most of all, he was fueled by railing against the BOT movement.

As he fumbled across the recess yard with a box full of leftover invitations, fresh sign-up sheets, copies of the meeting's agenda, and of course his prized wristlet, like a bolt of lightning he got a mental flash of Cleo at the BOT meeting. He imagined her struggling with the work that she had prepared for Benjamin's meeting, tripping and dropping things from a very similar box to what he was holding now as she ran behind Benjamin, thanklessly doing his bidding.

Sammy had judged Cleo so harshly then. Look at him now.

He quickly shook off any doubts and began justifying. He was different. Cleo was brainwashed by a lowlife, while Sammy was choosing to do this work. He could leave at any time. Indigo wasn't controlling him…

"Please hurry up, Sammy!" Indigo chirped from the other side of the recess area. "We already have GLO kids wanting to sign up!"

Sammy looked up over the top of his sunglasses to see a crowd forming around Indigo. She was standing on the same rock wall that the two of them had met on when first conceiving this idea.

The crowd was looking up at her with a mix of admiration and curiosity. As he neared the area, he could start to make out what she was saying.

"...and in *my* club, you will be able to make a difference! We can change the lives of so many of our fellow classmates through goodness, love, and opportunities for all. That's why we are called the GLO kids...G-L-O!" she said proudly.

Several members of the crowd clapped.

"I love this! This sounds amazing!" someone shouted from the audience.

My club? Indigo's words echoed through Sammy's mind. He didn't understand how she could take credit for a club they created together. Plus, he had put the actual nuts and bolts of it together basically by himself. And all of this was happening when he hadn't even made it over to the rock wall for the meeting yet?

Sammy's blood was starting to boil. He picked up the pace and quickly passed the crowd and slammed down the box on the rock wall next to Indigo's feet.

"With your donation of $20..." she paused and looked down at Sammy and whispered "thanks, bud" then continued.

BUD? Sammy's frustration was growing by the minute.

"With your donation, we will be able to help so many that need it. We are going to make sure that no one goes hungry, offering free school breakfasts for anyone who needs them!" The crowd cheered. "At lunch, we will offer special meal plans to accommodate everyone who has been overlooked, such as vegetarian and gluten-free options."

The clapping died down quickly on that one. Not many vegetarians in small-town America.

"We will ensure that each student has the school supplies that they need, so that everyone has the same chance to learn!" The crowd cheered louder. "We will make sure everyone has coats...no one will go cold as long as our warm GLO is around!" More clapping echoed around the schoolyard. "We are going to protect your rights from being taken from you. We will not submit to any uniform rules or tolerate terrible crimes like the unimaginable Locker Assault. The days of people like Benjamin Rosa pushing us around are over!"

The cheers had reached a fevered pitch. The audience's approval was growing with each new promise that Indigo offered.

Suddenly, a voice rose above the rest. "There's no way a small group of us kids can do all of that! And even if we could, who is paying for it?"

Sammy and Indigo both turned and noticed the originator of the dissenting comment. Of course. Middle of the Road "Roadkill" Ronald. Sammy couldn't understand what his problem was. Why couldn't he just pick a side already and go with it?

Indigo never broke stride and seamlessly flowed into a response. "I understand your point Ronald, and I hear you." She smiled. "Anything can be done if we work together!" She seemed to think that would satisfy him and turned to change the subject.

Ronald was undeterred. "But really, we can't pay for that! Even if you charge everyone $20, which is *way* more than the BOTs by the way, we wouldn't get anywhere close to being able to afford all of those promises. You can't just say something like that without a plan to back it up."

Indigo looked a bit more annoyed this time around, sneering through her smile. "Your opinions are valid Ronald and thank you for bringing them up. Put simply, the more GLO kids we can inspire to join our movement, the more money we will have to help people!"

Sammy anticipated this push-back on the GLO Club fee. While he had originally been against the BOT $5 entry fee, he now justified the higher GLO fee because they were aiming to help all kids, not just a small group of the school. He figured to help more kids you need more money.

Sammy saw Indigo struggling. He stepped up on the rock wall to join in the leadership of this meeting, a meeting that he thought was starting to get out of Indigo's control. He brought up a copy of his agenda to help get things *back on track*.

Bad choice of words.

He attempted to help. "Ronald, our plan is…" Suddenly he felt a hand on his shoulder. It was Indigo's.

"I'll handle this, Sammy. You can go hand out papers or…something." She motioned for him to step down off the rock wall. Sammy was in disbelief that he had just been dismissed like that.

"Listen Ronald," Indigo continued, "I'm sure it won't be a problem, however if we don't get enough voluntary registrations for the GLO club, I have a Plan B."

Plan B? What was she up to now?

Indigo continued. "If we have to, we will ensure that *every* student, not just GLO kids, are required to pay $20 each to make these services available to all students. After all, pitching in to help everyone is the only decent thing to do!"

A low rumble of chattering had started to gain momentum in the back of the crowd. Several BOTs had come to the meeting, and as he heard bits and pieces from their commentary, it was clear to Sammy that they were on a mission to sabotage the GLO agenda.

"What if we don't want a free breakfast or vegetable lunches?" yelled Cici. "Some of us like *real* food!" She laughed along with some of the other BOTs.

"You will be paying to help others who *do* want these things and can't have them yet. Don't you care about other kids?" Indigo asked, clearly starting to lose her cool.

"Of course, we do!" shouted Cici, this time more offended than before. "We just don't want to pay for something that we don't want or can't use — who will be paying for the things I want in life? Hey, I'd like some venison in the lunchroom. You know how I solve that?

I bring some in myself! I can bring some in after I go hunting this weekend if you all want," she said laughing.

"The point is that the GLOs will be a group of inclusion and helping. Anyone who doesn't want to help won't be very happy in our club I guess," Indigo said with a bite in her voice.

Sammy couldn't stand back anymore. He had to pipe up and get the meeting on the rails. He realized that Indigo's position on the wall, standing above everyone, was separating her from people. She was turning people off by seeming like she was talking down to them. He decided to speak from the ground, trying another approach.

"Settle down everyone and listen up!" He snapped his fingers in the air with sass, and many in the audience laughed. Only Sammy could get away with something like that. He now had their undivided attention.

"*Our* club, the GLO kids, simply want to help the school be better, and give love and tolerance where there isn't any. We are especially worried about the new movement going on, that shall remain nameless," he gave a feisty glance to the BOT kids in the back, "which is working to shut down people's freedom of speech to make us all roBOTs who are exactly the same!" He emphasized that last part of that "robot" word hard.

On purpose.

"Does that worry any of you?"

He saw some nodding in the audience. No one was shouting out, so he figured that quiet nods were the best he could ask for as proof that his points had been effective. "Cici! You mentioned wanting people to help you. What do you need?"

Cici was shocked at being called out, and equally flattered that Sammy was addressing her issues. "Well, um, I don't really need anything at the minute. I just meant that I don't want to pay for things that I won't use."

"That's fair," he said. "Then why join the club?"

"I probably won't," she said. "The BOTs seem to be a better fit for me."

Sammy kept talking, unsure and uninterested in what Indigo's reaction was behind him.

"Listen, if the BOTs seem like a better fit for you, go for it. You don't want the GLO kids to be in charge of using your money for things we think are best. I get it. We may not be right every time. But did you want to help rip down those locker signs the other week? Did that feel like something that helped everyone?"

"It sure didn't help me!" said Terri, whose locker defacing Sammy had witnessed firsthand.

He saw a tiny crack in Cici's tough demeanor, a look of slight shame come over her face at that minute. He felt emboldened.

"You really need to use your hearts to decide which club is the best for you! Do you want to be part of a group that is giving, or of taking? A group that is loving, or dividing? We as GLOs want to help those who can't help themselves, and we have a great plan of just how to do it!"

Just then, Autumn and Maryam stepped to the front of the crowd, their normally smiling and radiant faces looking pensive. Autumn spoke. "Have you asked any of the students if they actually *want* what you are planning to do for them?"

Sammy was caught off guard with that question. He had never been asked that before. He looked up to Indigo for insight, but her face just looked blank at the direction the meeting had gone. Sammy knew the responsibility was on him. He continued.

"Look, who wouldn't want free stuff? I know I do!" he said with a little sassy snap and hip bump, but the silence of the crowd communicated that this was no time for jokes. "Besides Autumn, I know you are a vegetarian, so why wouldn't you want this? We could make plant-based meals available to vegetarians like you and I and save animals in the process! Or don't you care about those sweet animals?" he said judgmentally.

"I'm not against helping animals *or* vegetarians!" she said emphatically. "And you're right that I have a special diet, but it isn't vegetarianism. I am kosher. My family is Jewish, and I can't eat the food from the school because I need it to be prepared a certain way."

"Then we can make sure the school has cashew food too!" Sammy said with a snip, rolling his eyes.

Several kids laughed. "Not cashew, kosher," Autumn said calmly. "And I don't need someone to bring my food to me, I will bring it myself. I would prefer that a club be helping with things like getting us new computers in the library so we can do our research papers or organizing a community clean up in the neighborhood around the school. This area is a mess and could use our help! Plus, it helps everyone."

"That's a great idea Autumn! We could do that too. What we need now is for everyone who is interested to sign up on…" Just then the bell rang. All the kids turned and started walking briskly towards the school.

Sammy stared at the mass exodus, completely deflated. He glanced down at the well-intended agenda that was now crumpled in his hand, the only one that had even been taken out of the box. He saw the sign-up sheets still in the box, with six different pens that he had brought for use by the masses of people he had expected to sign up.

He looked up at Indigo, now sitting on the rock wall. She looked like a balloon that had been popped by a pin. She was pitiable. But instead of sympathy, Sammy was angry.

Very angry.

"What were you thinking, Indigo?" he shouted. "I had a plan all worked out on this agenda, and then you start without me? You messed it all up! No one even understands what we want to do, or why we want to do it. This was so stupid!"

She looked down at her sandals, ashamed of how things turned out. "I'm sorry, Pepper, it's just that…"

"Stop calling me Pepper! We aren't friends! I don't even know why I did this with you. Now Cleo and stupid Bozomin will be laughing at us when they hear about this disaster!"

"Who is Bozomin?" Indigo said.

Oops.

"I didn't say that! I said *Benjamin*. Get your ears cleaned out." Sammy grabbed the box and its untouched contents and stomped away back to his locker, his gold shimmering "S" wristlet hooked over his wrist and swinging vigorously with each theatrical stomp.

ROADKILL

At this point, life was excruciating for Sammy. He still wasn't talking to Cleo, although they had resumed their awkward carpool to school. He knew that their parents were no longer falling for the tales of weeks-long food poisoning, or Cleo suddenly taking up full time residence at the church. It was obvious that something was awry between them, but everyone seemed to be assuming that things would get back to normal with the passage of time.

The interactions between Sammy and Cleo had devolved into trite pleasantries exchanged only during these rides to school. Sammy had been operating in such a mental fog lately, that when Reginald's beautiful black car rumbled down the driveway on this sunny day with the light sparkling off its fresh wax, he didn't even take notice.

The car came to a stop and Sammy jumped in.

"Hey," he said glumly.

"Hey Sammy!" Cleo said, almost chirping.

That friendly tone of hers, that sweet little nothing-is-wrong attitude infuriated Sammy. How could she not care one iota that their relationship was crumbling?

He couldn't believe Cleo would let years of friendship go down the drain without any fight at all. They still hadn't really had a real discussion about any of it. She hadn't even brought up his formation of the GLO club at all. The day she got back from the church retreat, he was anticipating her confronting him about it, so he had prepared by coming up with all sorts of witty retorts to anything she might say. And then she just…didn't…and he was as equally enraged at her lack of care about what he did.

Could it be possible that Cleo was unaware of how her membership in the BOTs, and subsequent actions as part of that club, had left him feeling betrayed and abandoned?

No. There was no way. She had to know. Not even Cleo could be that dense!

They rode the rest of the way in complete silence, with only the noise of Reginald's religious radio station minister speaking in the muffled background. Sammy just barely caught a few stray lines of that day's Bible story; something about the great friendship of Jonathan and David. But he quickly blocked it out, choosing to listen to his inner dialogue of fantasy arguments with Cleo on loop instead.

Today was the first time that the BOTs had a meeting scheduled on the same day as the GLO club. Sammy had not attended a GLO club meeting since the original debacle several weeks ago. He also had not spoken to Indigo, though she did regularly attempt to reach out to him.

With Sammy, you were either *in* or *out.*

Despite all odds, he'd let Indigo in. But after the way she'd dismissed Sammy's work and effort during the meeting, he felt that he had been fooled. She was now out.

Way out.

His guard was back up, and she'd have to pull off every magic trick short of raising Houdini himself to work her way back into his good graces.

On top of everything else, Ronald had been contemplating starting his own club. Sammy had suggested it be called the Roadkill Club, referring of course to Ronald's middle-of-the-road perspectives.

This seemed a fitting name, Sammy figured, since Ronald's centrist views were not only annoying, but social suicide.

Not surprisingly, Ronald had foregone that suggestion as well as the existing club acronym trend and instead planned to call his club the Compass Club, because he wanted people to choose their own directions for the group's work. He found this name to be very clever, and considering the number of times he worked it into a sentence, it was clear that he was quite proud of it.

"You kids are having a meeting today, right? What's your club called again?" Reginald smiled in the rear-view mirror, attempting to break the silence while unaware of the match he had innocently lit.

"Uh, actually dad, I'm in the BOT club. Sammy is in the GLO club."

"Wait, you two are in *different* clubs? Are there separate ones for boys and girls or something?" he asked, trying to make sense of this.

"No, dad, it's just that…"

"I'm not in *any* club," Sammy snipped.

Cleo looked over, now more confused than her father was. "You aren't?"

"I don't need to *buy* friends by joining any stupid club." Sammy sat with his arms crossed, making eye contact only with his own reflection in the car window.

Ever since Sammy's fall out with Indigo, Ronald had been working very hard to convince him to join the Compass Club. He hated to admit it, but Sammy agreed with a lot of Ronald's ideas. But he didn't take Compass very seriously. Most kids in school were aligning with either the BOTs or the GLO kids, and Sammy saw little reason to join an unknown club that stood for all the boring compromise stances.

If he was going to commit to any club (and at this moment, that is a big *if*) he wanted something exciting, something he could get passionate about, and to have a shared opponent with his fellow club members.

After all, what's wrong with a little us-and-them?

The second Reginald hit the brakes at the student drop-off, Sammy darted from the car, leaving Cleo behind as he entered the school briskly.

"Hey Sammy! Are you coming to our meeting today?" Sammy raised his gaze from the ground and saw Ronald ahead of him, holding the door open.

"Hey Ronald," he said blandly. He ignored the question, somehow hoping that Ronald had forgotten he asked it.

"*Well*? Are you coming? I'd love to count you in as a Compass kid!" he said hopefully.

"Ronald…" he sighed, trying to figure out how to say this kindly. "I don't think I'm going to join your Compass Club. Thanks anyway, though."

This is why Sammy hated in-person conversations, phones were so much better. Don't like talking to someone? *Bam*! Hang up and your problems are gone. Don't want to deliver in-person news? Type away and text it! Sammy's parents always said that in-person inter-actions were best, especially when giving tough news to someone. He disagreed, and during their heart-to-heart sessions with him he often wished he could hang up on them too.

In place of having a phone to hang up, he sped up his pace to hopefully lose Ronald in the hallway crowds.

"Sammy, wait!" He turned and saw Ronald was directly next to him. He was surprised how fast Ronald could run, since chess club was his only known cardio.

Sammy internally considered the logistics of starting a cartwheel race down the hall. He knew Ronald couldn't keep up with that, but then again, Sammy had just painted his nails the team colors for the big soccer game this weekend.

Didn't seem worth the manicure risk.

"You would be an awesome addition to the Compass Club!" Ronald paused, considering how best to tempt Sammy into joining. "We could host a gymnastics meet with you as the star, to raise money for the kids at the hospital who aren't as lucky as us to be healthy!" He smiled and looked at Sammy with hope.

Sammy continued walking briskly without responding. It did seem that hope alone wasn't going to work to stop Ronald's pursuit.

Ronald persisted doggedly, even as Sammy reached his locker and opened the door between their faces in another attempt to disengage. Ronald continued. "What about this? In May around Mother's Day, we could invite that mobile salon to the church and do a spa day for the moms and grandmas. They do so much for us, that it would be great to give back to thank the women that take care of us!" He looked on, smiling.

"Could we get mani-pedis ourselves?" Sammy closed the door halfway to make eye contact.

"I mean, I suppose maybe we could. We'd have to see if we have enough mo…"

Ronald suddenly sounded like the teachers in the old Peanuts cartoons. *Wah, wah, wah, wahhhh.* Sammy didn't hear a word he said after the implied yes.

Spa Day — now he was talking Sammy's language. Just then, the bell rang.

Sammy slammed his locker closed and ran from Ronald without a final verdict.

"So, can I expect to see you at the Compass Club meeting during recess?" Ronald said, faintly now as Sammy rushed into his classroom.

"Maybe! Talk to you later Ronald." And with that, Sammy dashed into his classroom. He smiled at Ms. Traben and then scowled at Benjamin the entire way down the aisle, flashing his nail polish as conspicuously as possible.

MIRROR

Sammy looked into the dingy mirror, his face illuminated with the hideous yellow glow of the fluorescent lights in the boy's bathroom. Sweat was now all over his forehead. He didn't mind a little glitter or glistening in his life, but sweat was definitely not welcome here. As he often did, he had snuck into the gym to burn off some of this nervous and frustrated energy that he was carrying around. This time he had grabbed a basketball and had played a very distracted game of HORSE with himself. He ran hard but wasn't focusing on the game at all. When he realized he had spelled out HOSE, he just gave up and left.

The goal had been achieved, he was exhausted and calmer, but also drenched in sweat, which he found to be a social embarrassment for the "most stylish kid in school," one of the many monikers he had given himself.

As he stood in the bathroom, dabbing up his sweat and changing into a purple iridescent T-shirt from the "emergency wardrobe" he kept in his locker, he stared into the mirror. He hadn't yet come to a decision about what to do regarding these clubs, and he thought staring harder into his own reflection in the mirror would do the trick.

He had a decision to make. Option one was that he could attend the GLO meeting with Indigo, and be her lapdog throughout the meeting, handing out papers or manning the sign-up sheet. That is, if she even bothered to have people sign up at all this time around.

This was an all-around shameful prospect. However, he agreed with much of what the GLO kids stood for, and he loved the idea of being a part of the rival group to the BOTs and devoting his time to taking down Benjamin.

His second option was to attend the Compass meeting with Ronald — he knew that would make Ronald's whole life. He probably agreed the most with Ronald's goals, but hardly any kids had joined the Compass Club, and he found Ronald's middle-ground views to be unmoving and bland. He saw compromise as a weak stance. Go big or go home!

His final option was to attend the BOT meeting. This option was unthinkable to Sammy, although he had considered, in his deepest moments of anger with Indigo, to join the BOTs and exact some form of revenge on her. Having her former partner join a club that her ex-boyfriend had started would surely teach her to regret what she lost.

Also, Sammy did enjoy the thought of being on the same side of something with Cleo again. But he didn't share many, if any, common beliefs with the BOTs or Benjamin and his cronies.

As Sammy stood there, imploring his own reflection to give him the answers he was seeking, the bathroom door flew open, and the chaotic hallway noise broke up his silent contemplation. His eyes moved to the reflection of the door in the mirror. As if this day couldn't get any more annoying...Benjamin walked into the bathroom.

"Hey, Sammy," Benjamin said. He started for one of the urinals but stopped and turned back. "I heard about the club you started with Indy."

"Indy?" Sammy of course knew who he was referring to but had chosen to give Benjamin a hard time about it anyway.

"Sorry, I meant Indigo. I just wanted to say that I think it is cool that you can be there to support her, especially if I can't. This was always the type of thing she wanted to get into, marching for causes and that type of thing. Good luck with all of that," he said with a gentle smile.

Sammy was not about to be fooled by his mocking disguised as an olive branch. Benjamin had to have heard about what a disaster the GLO meeting was and was here to rub it in Sammy's face.

All his hurt, embarrassment, abandonment, and resentment were starting to be more pressure than his inner dam of decency could hold back.

"We don't need your 'luck,' but thanks anyway," Sammy snapped.

Benjamin looked surprised. "Oh, I didn't mean anything by it. I just meant that I had heard you guys were starting a rival club to the BOTs, and I think it is good to see kids getting active over causes they are passionate about. At my last school…"

Sammy cut him off. "Look Boz…Benjamin. We don't need your help, we don't need your thoughts and prayers, we just need you to get out of our way. I wish you and your fellow roBOTs like Cleo good luck with '*your* club!'" he said, flashing air quotes.

Benjamin stood there, looking baffled by Sammy's ungracious reaction. It was clear that he was not used to people blowing him off. The surprise on his face made Sammy consider that he was actually being genuine in his comments.

Benjamin retorted, "I don't know what your problem is, but I was just trying…"

Just then the bathroom door flung open. Two of Benjamin's basketball teammates, Vinnie and Louie, walked in the door.

"Hey Benny!" one said. "What are you doing in here with this fruit cake?" he said, making a feminine hand gesture towards Sammy.

"Give him a break, guys," Benjamin said.

"Let's see who the fruit cake is when I, not any of you, am named the soccer MVP *again* at this year's banquet," Sammy clapped back. "I don't need to prove I'm tough by running around grunting like a pack of apes like you guys!"

Was it just his imagination, or did Sammy see a flicker of respect pass over the boys' faces as he glared at their reflections in the mirror? It was probably just a smudge on the glass.

He turned back to his wristlet, rummaging through it — not for anything in particular, but to look busy and disengaged from the conversation.

As Sammy continued to grope through the wallet, Vinnie bit back. "Oh, if you're looking for your manhood, I think you left it in your locker. Or wait, did Cleo throw that out for you when we threw out the rest of your crap?"

Watching them laughing, Sammy was infuriated beyond belief. He knew trying to physically fight three of them was useless, so he just kept up the wristlet-shuffle-charade.

Benjamin stepped in. "Forget it, let's go, guys." They started towards the door. "Oh, and again Sammy, good luck with your glee club," he said, intentionally mispronouncing the GLO club's name to impress his friends. They all laughed.

"I'll tell Cleo you said hi." Benjamin smiled.

Sammy was ready to erupt.

"Nice manicure, Maybelline." Louie chimed in as he exited with the others. All three looked over their shoulders as they walked out, laughing and exchanging insults about Sammy under their breath.

Sammy theatrically waved to them, palm down, wiggling his fingers to flash the nail polish directly at Benjamin. The door shut behind them. It was eerily silent in the bathroom now, with only Sammy and his reflection left alone, together. Again.

Sammy exhaled a breath of anger, frustration, and contempt. He felt his eyes welling up with tears at all the emotional negativity that his body was trying to process right now.

Negativity from without. Negativity from within.

He let out a long, guttural noise, a combination of a growl and a scream. Years of frustration came out of him in that moment, alone in the bathroom. He became unhinged. The pressure of the last few weeks was too much for him to handle. The loss of a best friend, of Cleo, his support system. The GLOs, the BOTs, the uniforms, the Locker Assault. Those dumb alpha-boys.

He began feverishly scratching at his nails, trying in vain to scrape off his beloved nail polish. He was embarrassed, annoyed, defiant, and compliant all at once. Try as he might, the scraping didn't work, as he of course bought only the best and longest-lasting brand. He scraped and scraped until his nail beds started to bleed. It was no use.

The nail polish was a part of him, just as the *desire* to wear nail polish was part of him too. In that moment, he felt resigned to who he was, resigned to the fact that people like Benjamin and his friends would never fully understand or accept him.

He struggled to rectify the part of him that didn't care an ounce what people like them thought, with the part of him that so deeply did. He had once had a friend that accepted him for exactly who he was.

But Cleo was gone now, and her departure felt like as much of a knife stab as Benjamin and his troupe of followers' verbal insults did to Sammy.

Actually, hers hurt much worse. And now it seemed she had abandoned him too.

He stared back at his face in the mirror, flushed cheeks, sweat beads on his forehead, tears in his eyes. He reached up to his face and wiped the streaks away with his hands, his blood-stained nail polish gleaming in the fluorescent glow of the bathroom lights.

Suddenly, a calm came over him.

His debate about the clubs had been answered. He had gotten the clarity he was looking for.

He knew now what he had to do.

A BLIND BAT

"Hey! You!" Sammy ran down the hallway, darting and weaving between the mass of kids leaving the lunchroom. "Indigo!"

As her head turned back, her long feather earrings slapped her in the face, almost as if they moved in slow motion. She looked back with a mix of optimism and confusion in her face. "Are you talking to me, Pep?"

Pep? Ugh, there she went again. He paused, realizing this was his last chance to change his mind.

"Pepper..." she stammered over herself, realizing her error. "Sorry...Sammy...did you need something?"

He looked down at her hands and saw her meekly holding some handwritten sign-up sheets, clearly in preparation for the GLO meeting today.

He didn't like what he saw. The writing was all crooked, she only used a blue pen — where was the panache in that! — and she didn't have an agenda. Again.

He turned his gaze up to her face, looking at her wide, hopeful eyes, which seemed to silently beckon him to come back and join the movement they had created together. She seemed to convey regret, apologies, and respect all at the same time. It was a silent exchange, but Sammy felt it.

He opened his mouth to speak. Indigo cut him off.

"Before you say anything, I wanted to say how sorry I am for how that first meeting went down," Indigo said, speaking rapidly like an auctioneer. She knew her groveling time was limited. "I just thought that we would have more time to lay out our GLO mission, but I got thrown off by the arguing. I didn't expect that, and I guess I'm not as good at handling those things on the spot as you are."

Sammy paused to allow her to continue her desperate petition to him. However, she didn't say anything further.

That was it? The punishment definitely didn't fit the crime.

"I wasn't so mad at your *horrible* handling of that meeting," Sammy said, not sparing a grain of salt for the wound. "It was a complete disaster for sure, and it was clear that you were struggling during the riot started by those big mouth BOTs. But I have been avoiding you for another reason."

She stood there, looking perplexed. He continued.

"How could you completely cut me out of the meeting? You called it *your* club, you told me to get down off the wall and go hand out papers, you acted like I was a servant. Like I was in your way, when I had done basically all the work. I won't be a part of something when I'm being disrespected like that."

Her eyes welled up with tears. "Oh my gosh! I had no idea! Oh Pepper, I'm so sorry, I didn't realize I did any of that. I am such a brute. Please forgive me."

Her groveling encouraged Sammy that things were headed in the right direction.

This was certainly changing the plans he had when he left the bathroom after his interaction with Benjamin.

So close, Ronald. Better luck next time.

"How do I know things will be different going forward?" he asked. "You could say this, and then just act the same again."

"Good question. You need assurances, I understand that. How about..." her eyes darted around the hallway.

"Okay, um, what if I give you a leadership role in the GLOs? Obviously, you are one of our leaders, but something with a title. If I'm the President, how about we make you Vice President?"

Sammy didn't like having a title that was in deference to another person. He had no plans to be someone's dumpy sidekick. He needed something with real power.

He paused to consider the options. Leader? Nah, too generic. Deputy? Sounds official, but he wasn't entirely sure what it meant. Then he settled on one.

"I want to be the GLO Club Director, and I will bring on other Assistant Directors to help me, and we will do the work of the club, and you can be the face and share the message."

Sammy figured that a blind bat would have an easier time finding its way out of a pillowcase than Indigo would figuring out what this club really needed. He also knew that she may be confused about the offer at first — why would he do all the work while she got all of the glory? At least that was how she'd see it. But Sammy knew where the real power was. She was the show horse, he was the work horse — like a puppeteer pulling the strings from behind the curtain.

He was liking this proposal more as he thought it through.

"I'm in! Are you back in too?" She started goofily clapping her hands quietly in front of her face, smiling like a cat that had just caught a canary. She clearly felt victorious.

Sammy, however, knew with this arrangement who undeniably controlled the GLO kids now.

"Sam-my, Sam-my," she whisper-chanted, continuing with her silly clapping.

He had to put a stop to this.

"Let's do this," he said with a smirk.

Her face erupted with joy. "Sammy! You won't regret this! We are going to have the best time!"

"Simmer down, girl," Sammy said sassily. He hated desperation, and her excitement was so over the top that it almost made him change his mind on the spot. But the path had been blazed. And it was worth it.

She interlocked arms with him, and they walked briskly outside, to the playground to launch the new GLO Club during recess. Together.

FEEDING THE BEAST

During the next few weeks, things escalated dramatically. Both clubs, still flying under the radar of most EHS adults, had begun a childish game of tit-for-tat, back and forth. Everyone was hyper-focused on being "right," getting in the last word, and ensuring that their club *appeared* to be the most generous and mission driven.

After all, appearances are everything in politics.

After the Locker Assault, the newly reunited GLO Club convinced the administration to make everyone attend a Sensitivity Training Assembly. It was billed as a community-building event, complete with a panel of "experts" with Indigo's dad, Dante, among them. Once the adults finished, the GLOs took the stage with their lineup of Locker Assault "survivors." Each speaker told their story in escalating levels of drama until finally, Sammy — naturally — closed it out with the emotional mic-drop moment.

By the end, the BOTs were seething. They called an emergency meeting to discuss what they called a "scripted sob-fest" designed to make them look like villains. Benjamin led the charge, fuming about the "farce" and vowing revenge. His plan: the BOTs would finally deliver on their campaign promise to create paid "club jobs."

First on the list? Spy.

Training for the new spies didn't exactly go smoothly. GLO members caught them more than once — lurking in bushes, taking photos while wearing fake mustaches, or, in Cici Bubber's case, crouched behind a tree line in full hunting camo.

Effective in the woods; not so great on a manicured playground.

The GLOs were outraged and tattled to the faculty, but no one seemed to care. To the adults, these club wars were still seen as harmless fun. So, the GLOs decided to fight fire with fire. If the BOTs wanted spies, they'd have spies too — just unpaid ones, since they'd already made a big public fuss about how "immoral" the idea was.

It became their little secret, whispered in hallways and carried out in code. Because if you're going to spy, you might as well excel at it.

Things just continued to go further downhill. Benjamin arranged for the limo from his family's country club to show up at EHS one day with Indigo and Sammy's photos taped to the side. The unflattering enlarged photos of their heads accompanied a sign that said:

Paid for by your GLO dollars.
YOU pay more so WE get more!

He had also taped fake dollars all over the car and had tied more of them from strings that dangled off the back of the bumper.

Benjamin's big plan to humiliate them at recess backfired. Thanks to a scheduling mistake, Sammy and Indigo found out about the prank while they were at lunch. The timing flop killed the drama, but not the gossip. Half the school had seen it, and the rest heard about it through the ever-reliable EHS grapevine.

On Benjamin's birthday, Indigo and Sammy mobilized the GLO members, as well as many of their non-club friends and Sammy's soccer teammates, to dress in black clothing from head to toe. As participating students entered school that day, Sammy and Indigo handed them signs to wear around their necks that said:

THE NEW WE

RIP to Diversity: Welcome to BOT World!
*Join us in a **silent** day of obedience, where we all look the same,*
hide our personalities, and keep quiet as Benjamin likes it.
Happy Birthday to our favorite Dictator!

Of course, the BOTs weren't about to let it slide. Later that week, the GLO Club announced their first weekday event, "Talk and Tea," a casual after-school meetup at the local coffee shop to chat about club topics. The day before the event, Benjamin struck back — slipping fake invitations into every locker. His version read *Girls' Night Out!* and featured the same hideous limo photos of Indigo and Sammy, now with dresses crudely drawn over their bodies and Sammy's rainbow shoes and painted nails front and center.

Tit for tat. Back and forth it went.

Then came the speeches.

Anyone would agree that Benjamin and Indigo were both engaging and charismatic speakers, even if they couldn't stay on topic to save their lives. They had the ability to rally a crowd, sell a platform, and spin a message to their benefit.

Benjamin was the King of Spin. Whenever someone called him out — whether for his outbursts during speeches or for actions that didn't match his religious faith or the BOTs' mission — he'd flip the script. Instead of defending himself, he'd point fingers at Indigo and the GLOs, reciting a list of their supposed "offenses." He never felt the need to explain or even admit what he'd done; distraction was his favorite defense.

"I'm not sure what you are referring to when you talk about the BOTs 'defacing lockers,' but what I *know* is shocking, is how Indigo wasted half of the GLO money in the first few months to donate and fund events at the refugee center that Maryam is part of. *One* kid here is a refugee! Why is that our priority? How does that help the simple locals like you and me? Indigo and the GLO kids don't care about *us*!"

On the other hand, Indigo was the Queen of Martyrdom. At a base level, she employed very similar tactics to Benjamin's, though hers were more subtle. Her sleight-of-hand moves involved less finger-pointing, and more implications of misdeeds of the BOTs through her own positive actions.

"Look friends, I am a peaceful leader. I don't need to go out and destroy your property or take away your rights to feel powerful. In fact, if I had my way, *any* club that did things like that would be eliminated for what they have inflicted on our school. We have *suffered* at the hands of bullies for too long. Now, though, the GLOs will ensure that we have a tolerant, peaceful, and loving world for all students! Well...except for certain you-know-whos..." Indigo giggled, and the crowd cheered at the "unmentioned" BOT mention.

A particularly regrettable side effect of the hateful rhetoric being spewed by both clubs was the division that grew among friends: Sammy and Cleo, Terri and Megan, Indigo and Benjamin, Ronald and...well, everyone.

Slowly, the clubs were turning into hungry beasts — always needing to be fed, their appetites growing, their demands multiplying. The students were running out of ways to keep them satisfied. And when the food ran out, the beasts might just devour *everyone*.

CLEO

For the first time since she could remember, Cleo wasn't having a birthday party. For weeks, her father had been offering to plan one for her. He had suggested they go to the zoo again, knowing how much fun she had last year with Sammy and her church friends, studying the animals, playing with the face paint, and living as close as a young lady could get to her future dream: being a veterinarian.

Or, Reginald proposed, he could arrange a bowling outing with the entire Arco family, and of course Sammy.

Double yay.

Neither Reginald nor the Iris parents fully grasped the distance that had wedged itself between these former best friends. For Cleo, the thought of having a party with Sammy at this point seemed improbable.

But the thought of having a party *without* him was inconceivable.

She decided to avoid a party altogether so that she wouldn't need to address the situation at all. Cleo felt a familiar rumbling in her stomach. She knew it was stress from everything going on at school and at home. She preferred to avoid conflict, but was it worth it to let the issues between Benjamin and Sammy prevent her from having a birthday party?

As she sat there in the pew, staring blankly up at the beautiful stained-glass windows and running through the scenes in her mind from last year's birthday party with a mix of happy and sad sentiments, she glanced up at her father who was now walking to the pulpit to deliver a reading.

Cleo knew that nothing was more important to her father than ensuring that she walk the same path of faith he did. Daydreaming during church was strictly prohibited, and somehow, her father always knew when she did. She loved her father for how understanding and kind he could be, but sometimes his inflexibility when it came to her commitment to church was a little exhausting.

As he settled in at the pulpit, arranging his Bible and papers, Cleo was snapped out of a daydream as he shot her a disapproving look, complete with a pursed lip. She shot up like a ramrod in the pew, partly to convince her father of how attentive she was, partly to motivate herself to ensure that this was actually true. She knew she'd be hearing critiques of her inattentiveness tonight.

"A reading from Colossians 3:13. 'Bear with each other and forgive one another, if any of you has a grievance against someone. Forgive as the Lord forgave you'..."

While she had already started daydreaming again, she had to admit that those were an impactful 10 seconds. Every word of that reading spoke to her in that moment.

She knew that she should bear with Sammy. He went through a lot, being as unique as he was. She just didn't understand why he had been so angry lately, just because she wanted to be a part of a club with some church friends?

She perked back up to feign continuing interest in her father's ongoing words.

"...and so, we need to bear with our friends, as they may have struggles that we know nothing about." Reginald continued speaking in his melodic tone and pace, emphasizing the most impactful words, and pausing effortlessly to allow points to settle.

"Few struggles reach the light of day." He looked around the room, making direct eye contact with members of the congregation. "In fact, most remain hidden in darkness. Think about it…are there many people that know your deepest struggles? I'd bet there aren't. That's true for most of us. How well do we know *anyone*? Really think about it…" He tapped his head as he asked them to think, then walked silently across the stage, allowing the silence to permeate the room. He settled in back at the pulpit.

"Today, I ask all of you to find forgiveness and empathy for your family, friends, and for strangers too," he paused, looking around the room to take in all of the new and old faces in the room, "…because you know *nothing* of the silent struggles they face every day, just as they know nothing of *yours*."

Cleo smirked. Maybe her father was right. Maybe she should pay attention more often. This was some good stuff.

She could see how joining forces with Benjamin, someone who Sammy had built up in his mind as his archenemy, could be difficult for him to accept. But she also knew that Sammy dramatically over-emphasized any offense that Benjamin had ever done to him, or any real problem that Benjamin actually had with Sammy.

Did Sammy *really* think that she would be friends with someone who was cruel or hating towards her friends? Could he think that little of her?

She paused, knowing from Sammy's recent behavior that the answer seemed to be "yes."

The thing was, Cleo wasn't even that passionate about Benjamin or the BOT Club, which is what made this even more painful. She was losing her best friend mainly to make her dad happy.

Benjamin was a nice enough guy, but not Cleo's cup of tea when looking for a friend. However, his parents, Didi and Wyatt, were big donors to the church. The standing ask to any Arco family member was to "show gratitude" at all times — *especially* to any member of the Rosa family. So here Cleo was…gratitude-ing. Like it or not.

But now, Sammy's reaction was causing her to dig in her heels and defend Benjamin. It was the principle of the thing.

She knew that just by virtue of being Sammy, that he would never make the first move towards reconciliation. But she could also see how she had contributed to the problem and was thankful for these few quiet daydreaming moments at church to ponder the situation and gain some clarity.

Now, she had to figure out what to do with it.

* * *

Each week after church services, Cleo and the other members of the youth group, including Benjamin, gathered in the church basement for lunch and socializing. As the minister's daughter, Cleo was normally in charge of serving and cleaning up the food. Today, however, she had been given the day off by her father because it was her birthday.

"What's that kid's problem with me?" Cleo turned around to see Benjamin standing there, fiddling with the Bible Study felt board hanging in the hallway.

"Who?" Cleo was confused.

"Sammy. What does he have against me? I've never done a thing to the guy! Other than tell him to leave his fruity flame pants at home," he laughed.

"See, but it is things like that. He feels bullied by you. Maybe you could lay off him a little bit."

"Whoa, whoa. *I* need to lay off *him*? Sammy is a pit bull! That guy doesn't get ruffled by anything. I feel like he is coming at me every day, on the attack over every little thing. I have no choice but to push back! Can you imagine if I didn't stand up for myself? What would the other guys say?"

"Sammy seems strong, but he is sensitive. When guys like you pick on him, it makes him feel like an outsider. If you tried to be kinder, turn the other cheek, maybe you two could be friends." Cleo smiled at the far-fetched thought.

"*Guys like me?*'" Benjamin repeated, looked frustrated.

"You know what I mean. Alpha guys. Jocks. Popular guys."

"Oh, cool. I'll take that as a compliment. The thing is, I don't have a problem with the guy, but if he keeps this up, I cannot be held responsible for what I say. I'm *not* going to let him walk all over me. It's bad enough how much my dad grills me about how much better Sammy is in soccer than me. I need to maintain some shred of pride!"

Cleo heard rustling in the common room, a sure-fire sign that birthday antics were underway. "I need to go in here for my birthday thingy now. You want to come in with me?" she said with a roll of her eyes. Benjamin shrugged, still clearly focused on his own problems.

As she stood outside of the door to the rec room, she took a deep breath of preparation. It was obvious to her that they were all going to pop out and yell "surprise!" or something equally as embarrassing. Her dad meant well, but she just wasn't in the mood for this.

She knew it was time to bust out her acting chops.

Before entering the room, she began practicing the part, covering her mouth and bulging her eyes out in faux shock. *"Oh my gosh! I didn't expect this at all! You almost gave me a heart attack! Thank you to everyone...wow what an unexpected surprise!"* Her face dropped to the resting sadness that was permeating her birthday today.

That'd have to do.

Benjamin opened the door first and held it open for Cleo. She entered with a flourish, and...nothing. Looking around the room, it seemed that no one remembered the significance of today. There were no balloons, no presents, no cake, no huddled mass of whispering students in the corner conspicuously attempting an obvious surprise. This was a big relief to Cleo, because this year she just felt sad and exhausted. She missed her best friend, she was overwhelmed with the amount of work that Benjamin had her doing for the BOTs, and the most emotionally draining thing of all was...Genevieve.

Cleo had no memory of her father ever dating anyone. He had always been a single dad as far back as she could remember. Cleo was unsure if he had truly never found anyone that was a good match for him, or if his commitment to being the best father to her during her younger years was what had resulted in his solitary life.

Either way, it looked like things were changing.

Since Reginald had coupled up after her beef with Sammy had already started, Cleo hadn't even had an opportunity to tell Sammy about Genevieve yet.

She was a young widow who had lived a rather quiet life, but now, as dashing Reginald's girlfriend, she was the center of attention. Like it or not.

Reginald Arco was the most magnetic force in this small-town church, and as far back as Cleo could remember, every church lady within twenty-five miles seemed to want his ring on her finger.

She looked over at Genevieve, surrounded by fawning church ladies, and was nauseated at the ridiculous and insincere scene. They might as well ask for her autograph.

Watching this, Cleo couldn't help imagining what Sammy's snarky commentary would be. He'd probably say they all looked like crazy chickens clucking around the head hen, he'd mock the middle-aged desperation, and he would *definitely* critique the group's questionable fashion choices. Cleo smiled — really smiled — for the first time in months.

She had not figured out what was so special about Genevieve to bring Reginald out of a years-long dating drought, and it seemed the rest of the church ladies wanted to understand the same thing.

They clamored for her attention, and peppered her with endless questions about her past, her faith, even questions about her reproductive health. Apparently, her ability to "breed" with their leader was a top priority to these total strangers.

Cleo's contempt mixed with pity. In some ways, she felt bad for her, being treated like a Holstein cow up on the auction block being evaluated for sale. She watched Genevieve as she deflected comments and judgments like a knight holding a sword and shield fighting off opponents. Cleo marveled at her mastery.

Genevieve seemed to take it all in stride, at least from the outside.

Her adjustment to the life of a Presbyterian minister's girlfriend had been a fairly seamless one, but the biggest change was the presence of a child, Cleo. She had never raised a child before, and Cleo had never had a mother figure, so the two of them were navigating new terrain both together, and at odds. But more than anything, Cleo struggled with the loss of one-on-one time with her dad.

This played a big part in why Cleo had thrown herself headfirst into her work with the BOTs. Having something to do that kept her mind busy on nights and weekends was a large help over these last months. Neither her friendship with Sammy, nor her relationship with her dad, felt like home anymore.

Oh, and her singing! Cleo smiled again, thinking of the funny things Sammy would say about Genevieve's terrible singing during the family's fireside piano hymn singalongs. She remembered back to the years when Sammy would come and enjoy her family's holiday gatherings around a piano, where everyone singing hymns, patriotic anthems, or anything else that the season called for. Once or twice, Cleo had caught Sammy nearly moved to tears due to the nostalgic and old school nature of it.

Not that he admitted to those tears. He told her they were "sudden allergies."

Reginald had been the family's go-to piano player before Cleo became proficient. She loved growing up with music and had vowed to carry on the family tradition. Though she was nowhere near Reginald's ability, he swelled with pride at her interest in carrying on this special piece of their family history.

Unfortunately, now that Genevieve was around, the spotlight had been stolen from Cleo and was firmly on "Viv" (as Genevieve asked to be called), and not for the reasons Viv would hope for. Her impassioned singing was a perplexing mix of half-operatic vibrato, half cat-on-a-hot-tin-roof yelping. Cleo had worked through every conceivable strategy for broaching the topic with either her father or Viv herself, but there is just no way to tell someone that your singing, the activity you enjoy more than anything else in life, is worse than the sound of a dying hyena.

Cleo had been having play-conversations in her mind with Sammy, imagining the barbs they would exchange about the topic, and the hyena joke was one that his imaginary self had delivered to her imaginary amusement.

Just then, the lights in the church basement went off. Cleo recognized her father's jazzy freestyle way of playing the piano, as the sound began to ring across the room.

"Happy Birthday, to you..." he started out singing alone in his low, gravelly voice, but soon enough the whole room chimed in. Cleo noticed something, or actually, the absence of something. Where was Viv's squawking? Suddenly a faint light glowed in the corner of the room. Viv came over, carrying a huge sheet cake, cawing all the way, with her huge smile and glittering eyes illuminated by the candles.

Cleo was mortified. Who did this woman think she was to bring Cleo her birthday cake? She had only known her a few months! Why was her dad all the way across the room? She glanced down at the cake to see a photo that had been printed into the icing, a group photo of the entire family from last year's zoo party. While there were nearly a dozen loved ones pictured, she saw only one face in the cake: the smiling mug of Sammy front and center with his face paint, his sequin party hat, and his "Queen Cleo" T-shirt that everyone had been given as a party favor. Her eyes welled up with tears.

Sammy had made it to her birthday, but not the way she had hoped he would. So much was changing!

Sammy wasn't here, Viv *was* here, everything was just backwards and mixed up!

Cleo couldn't take it. She covered her face to hide the tears that were forming in her eyes and ran out of the room. As she ran out, she heard her father's playing, along with his singing voice, fade out to a stunned silence.

BENJAMIN

"Man-up Benny!" Benjamin's dad Wyatt kicked a ball to his son who was playing goalie in the family's home soccer net. The ball flew by Benjamin's head like a rocket into the goal. Wyatt brushed back his sun-kissed blonde hair with pride and began an obnoxious victory dance.

Benjamin rolled his eyes, knowing what was coming next.

"Bulldog, bulldog, bow, wow, wow! Don't mess with a Yale man, baby!" Wyatt laughed and punched Benjamin's shoulder as he ran by.

Humility wasn't in Wyatt's vocabulary.

Benjamin's dad made a lot of money in the stock market over the years, which he had parlayed into a very successful real estate empire, specializing in luxury homes across the state. In this area of rural Pennsylvania, luxury homes were not exactly prevalent. Because he was the only game in town for ritzy homes, he had carved out a rather large empire in the western part of the state, owning the rural luxury market from Pittsburgh to Erie and even crossing the state border into Ohio to Cleveland and Columbus.

The Rosas lived on one of the largest and most sprawling estates in Emerald, with a pool, tennis court, and soccer field, where father and son practiced during Benjamin's mandatory coaching sessions with his father.

"This must be embarrassing for you, huh? An old man wiping the floor with you…I thought I had a son *and* a daughter, not *two* daughters," he said with a condescending chuckle.

"There's nothing wrong with being like a girl!" Benjamin's mom Didi yelled snippily from the open kitchen window.

"Of course not!" Wyatt said cheerily. He turned to Benjamin and whispered, "unless you are my *son* acting like one!" He turned and dove to kick another goal.

"So, what's all this I hear about that gay kid Sammy beating you in soccer? How is that possible? With the two of you on this team I have to wonder, are there any *real men* playing for EHS at all?"

"We *are* real men, Dad. And I don't know if Sammy is gay or not, but who cares? He's an awesome player and deserves to be the captain. You can't argue with his stats. He never even practices, that's all natural. He's incredible."

Wyatt grumbled. "Well, that may be true, but I imagine if you buckled down that you could show him who's boss. Then you could get him to stop wearing that ridiculous nail polish during games." He shook his head in disgust, while sinking one goal after another with the only ball they had taken to the field, leaving Benjamin to stand there pointlessly. "How can they allow this? In my day, men dressed and acted like men. Is that too much to ask?"

"Hardly anyone cares about that stuff anymore, Dad," Benjamin said quietly.

"Well, I do! This whole country is falling apart. Speaking of that, how are things going with the Back on Track team? Are you and that Black girl having any luck drumming up business?"

"Dad…don't call her tha…" he sighed in defeat. "We are called the BOT Club. "It's going pretty good. We have about 25 members now."

"Off to a good start, but you can do better. How are things going for the glee club with Sammy and that Spanish girl you dated? Indiana?"

Benjamin sighed at how many things were wrong in that last sentence. "They are the GLO Club, her name is Indigo, she's not Spanish, she's Latina, and they are doing well too. Their club is a little bigger than ours, but after our next meeting we will get enough sign ups to be bigger than they are again."

"He's beating you at this too? Maybe I should bring Sammy home as my new second daughter instead of you. At least he'd be a winner!"

Benjamin couldn't bring himself to look up from the ground. He didn't want to make eye contact with his father. He felt embarrassed, angry, resentful, and misunderstood.

Just then, his little sister came running outside. Her blonde ringlets bounced under a crooked tiara as she romped through the yard, tripping over her pink princess gown, and twice dropping her fairy wand. A huge smile washed across Benjamin's face.

Little Alice was his favorite person in the world. He was her idol too — when she looked at him, he felt embraced by all the admiration and love that he didn't usually feel from *certain* other members of his family.

He scooped her up and left his dad at the soccer net alone, scoring goal after goal and congratulating himself by making crowd noises after each one.

Benjamin took his sister inside and plopped her down on the couch. "Want to play princess with me?" she said with hope in her eyes. Benjamin skeptically pondered the thought of putting on a princess dress and makeup, especially considering the conversation he had just had with his father.

"Maybe in a little bit. Why don't you help mom with dinner?"

"Why don't *you* help mom with dinner?" his mom Didi said. "I could use another hand with these burgers."

The way Benjamin saw it, his mom was perfect at being what everyone expected — the kind of mom who always looked nice, smiled for the neighbors, and kept the house just right. She came from a rich family, and her dad used to tell her that money was the most important thing for feeling safe. Even though Benjamin didn't totally get it, he could tell his mom had come to believe that.

He'd once heard his Aunt Tina say that his mom had been deeply in love with someone before his dad. They met in college, and she'd been really happy back then. But she broke up with him before graduation when she met his dad, Wyatt. While she didn't have the same love for him, Wyatt was solid, dependable — the kind of person that her parents said was "a good choice."

But every now and then, especially when they were at church during one of Reginald's sermons, Benjamin would notice his mom smile for a second, while her eyes went distant and filled up with tears, like she was remembering something she couldn't quite say. Sometimes he wondered if she was thinking about that other man, the one she never talked about.

"Do you mind if I run upstairs and give Cleo a quick call about tomorrow's meeting? Dad can take the burgers out to the grill. He's not doing anything else productive, believe me," Benjamin said with a bite.

"Okay, you can call Cleo. And…" she put her hand on his shoulder, "just ignore your dad. He doesn't show love easily — no one knows that better than me! He tries to be tough, but please know that he is really proud of you, Benny. And so am I, love. Try to let his comments roll off your back, that's what I do!" Didi plastered on her empty Stepford-wife smile and turned back to the kitchen.

Benjamin kissed his mom's head and looked over at Alice. "Be back in a few minutes, squirt." He ran his hand over her face, mussing up her hair. He heard her giggling as he ran upstairs.

Benjamin never would've guessed he and Cleo would end up friends. She was quiet, obedient, basically everything that he was not. But lately, he'd started to respect that — especially when it came to the BOTs. The whole idea had started during one of their weekend church retreats, sitting by the campfire, complaining about how nobody at Emerald seemed to care about rules or tradition or faith anymore.

That talk had stuck with him, especially after what happened to his little sister.

Alice was in first grade — tiny, cheerful, and way too trusting. On her last birthday, she'd worn a brand-new princess skirt she'd been begging for, and it was her prized birthday gift that year. As she twirled down the hallway, her skirt puffing out like a parachute, she bumped into a fourth grader named Bart and sent his clay art project crashing to the floor.

Bart laughed at first. Then, in front of his friends, he shoved her into a locker and leaned on the door while she cried and banged to get out. When he finally wandered off, she crawled out, hands scraped, skirt streaked with black locker grease, and her birthday… ruined.

When the Rosas had reported the incident to the administration, the school had done an investigation, but they couldn't corroborate Alice's story, so no disciplinary action was taken.

Bart's dad called it "boys will be boys." Benjamin called it the last straw.

He'd always thought his old religious school was too strict — uniforms, curfews, a rule for everything. But now, Emerald felt like the Wild West. Nobody seemed to care, not even when a kid hurt his sister.

That's when the idea for the BOTs really took shape. If the adults wouldn't enforce order, maybe the students could.

Maybe *he* could. An eye for an eye, he thought. That was fair. Wasn't it?

Benjamin belly-flopped onto his bed and grabbed his phone. He opened his favorites list and hit Cleo's name, waiting as the phone rang. She didn't answer.

That was odd, because she knew that they had a call planned for today. Cleo never misses a BOT appointment. Then again, after that birthday cake disaster at the church earlier, she was probably hiding somewhere throwing darts at Viv's photograph.

He tried her phone again. Voicemail. *What is going on?* he thought.

He pulled up the texts and shot her a note. *"Hey. Where are you? Dad's being annoying as always. Hope your day is going better than mine. Let me know when we can talk about BOT stuff. HBD. -B."*

Benjamin tossed his phone on the end table in frustration and heard a deafening thud. He looked down to the ground to see that he had knocked a large crystal to the ground, a piece of Labradorite to be exact. Panicked, he rushed to pick up the stone and began examining it for damage or cracks. His heart slowed as he saw that everything seemed to be intact.

Back when they were dating, Indigo had given him this stone. He spent hours holding it up to the lamp, watching its green, yellow, and blue flash in the light. She had told him that it was a Heart Chakra stone and would help him to connect with his emotions better. She had hoped that this would allow him to open up more freely so he could be more "emotionally available" in his relationships.

At the time, Benjamin knew that it wasn't really a compliment, more of an attempt to fix him with energy healing, so he hadn't given it much thought. But now that they were broken up, he clung to this stone both literally and figuratively as one of the last pieces of their relationship.

He stared at the crystal, illuminating the flash in the sunlight, all the while wondering what Indigo was doing right now.

Was there anything he could do to get her back? This thought consumed much of his day. Every day.

Just then, Alice burst into the room. She had changed dresses and now had on a long, blue princess gown and glittery slippers. She had clearly done her own makeup, as her darling features were accentuated with vibrant streaks of misplaced enhancements everywhere. She had red lipstick streaked up her cheeks, mascara smeared around her eyelids and upper cheeks, and green eyeshadow on her lips. He couldn't help but laugh at this sight.

"Why hello, miss lady!" Alice said, motioning to Benjamin. "Oh of course, I would *love* to give you princess lessons!" she said, carrying on a one-sided conversation. "Let's begin with your makeup!" She came closer to him, took off her pointed hat, which had a long scarf hanging from it, and an elastic chin strap. She placed the hat on Benjamin and looked at her brother with joy. "Now, let's begin with the eyes." She pulled out the mascara brush and began dragging it across his eyelids. The rough brush hurt with each stroke, but he didn't have the heart to tell her so.

"Thank you, princess," he said. "You are good at this."

"Of course," she said. "I am a princess, and we are *very* good at being beautiful."

Benjamin's phone jingled. He looked down and saw a note from Cleo.

"Hiding in car. Dabbing blood from my ears. Viv is inside singing again. Disaster. Talk tomorrow. HBD to me."

"No phones in Alice's Kingdom!" Alice reprimanded. She took the phone and put it far away on the dresser. She threw the still-open mascara tube on the ground, leaving a black mark on the rug. She erroneously reached for the lipstick and began drawing lines on her brother's cheeks, babbling on about the importance of blush.

Just then, Wyatt walked into the room.

He stood there, smirking at the scene. Benjamin couldn't tell if he was disgusted at Benjamin or amused at little Alice's skills and imagination. He didn't have to wonder long.

He shook his head. "My two daughters," he said judgmentally, and walked out of the room.

SQUAD AND BRIGADE

Sammy was exhilarated.

He was reveling in building his little GLO army. Though he was a pacifist when it came to real war, the power that he was feeling from the creation of his team of club soldiers was…empowering. Exciting. Addicting.

He took a silent sip from his chai latte as Indigo kicked off the first of these sure-to-be painful weekly club leadership meetings. Here at his favorite coffee shop, sitting beside Indigo and across from Benjamin and Cleo, things couldn't be more awkward.

"Sammy, can you share your report about the Squad?" Indigo's voice snapped him out of a daydream.

"Oh, sure. Uh, I have recruited five kids so far that I'll supervise as GLO Leaders. We are calling them the Squad. So far, they include Terri, Maryam, Autumn, and the Bailey brothers, Bruce and Matthew."

Terri was the first one to jump at the opportunity to join in on the GLO leadership, as her resentment for the BOTs had been building since Benjamin and Cleo had raided her locker. She had an axe to grind and was ready to be Sammy's little pit bull should he need her.

He definitely planned to need her.

Maryam and Autumn maintained their frustration with the vagueness of the GLO club's goals, but Sammy had convinced them that the club needed their participation to help create guidelines and structure for the club. They liked the idea of being able to mold it into something that made sense, because they did agree with the tentpoles of what Sammy and Indigo were trying to do.

"The Bailey brothers? How did you get those two away from their video games to do something like this?" Benjamin looked both impressed and perplexed.

Matthew and Bruce were two of Sammy's and Benjamin's fellow soccer teammates. While they were mildly interested in what the GLO club stood for, more than anything they had joined the club to meet girls.

Well also, Sammy had leveraged his role as the captain of the soccer team when presenting the "opportunity" for them to serve on the leadership of the club as more of a command than a request.

And as we know, no one can say no to the Pepper.

"They jumped at it! I didn't have to do anything at all. I guess the GLO Club sells itself," Sammy said, hoping to taunt Benjamin with their participation.

In addition to heading up the Squad, Sammy had also self-nominated himself to draft the GLO Constitution. The Squad section declared:

Neither the current President, nor any GLO President going forward, may make decisions without a majority of the Squad approving it. When vacancies exist on the Squad, these leaders will be replaced with new students that other GLO members vote in.

This first time around, though, Sammy had populated the Squad with leaders of his own choosing. If he had his way, he would keep these current members in their roles for as long as possible. He felt he had a ton of control and influence over these particular students, which he relished.

Sammy was positioned exactly where he wanted to be — the leader of the leaders. Without Indigo even realizing it, Sammy had developed a role for himself that had more influence than any of the other leaders, or even Indigo herself.

Benjamin taunted, "looks like your little pep Squad is doing a bang-up job. I saw that you guys blew most of your money donating to that refugee center fundraiser. What were you thinking, using your money on such a niche thing?"

"It isn't niche, it is important!" Indigo was getting more and more annoyed at the continual judgment of these charitable events.

It took all Sammy's might to zip his lips so this meeting kept moving along. He had to get out of this. He looked at his watch impatiently.

Speaking of charity, the GLOs were at it again — hosting another feel-good event right here at the coffee shop. Tonight's theme? *Green Tea for a greener EHS.* The fundraiser would support their newest project: an Environmental Club at school that promised cleanups, recycling drives, LED lights, and refillable water stations to save the planet one hallway at a time.

For every tea sold, half the profit went straight to the cause. And Sammy had already assigned himself the role of unofficial bouncer — no one was leaving without a steaming cup of matcha and a donation receipt in hand.

He was more than ready to wrap up this meeting of the enemies. And fast. He had zero interest in refereeing this lover's quarrel.

Sammy picked up his phone and texted Matthew to be sure that he would be in attendance to document tonight's event for the school news. At these types of charitable events, Sammy felt it was impor-tant for the GLO kids to capture photos of themselves to "get credit" for their charitable nature. Matthew was a fantastic photographer, but Sammy was getting increasingly frustrated when reviewing his work, as most of the photos from his shoots were simply useless images of girls, girls, and more girls.

"By the way, what is going on with Cici? You need to get her under control, Benny. She has been a live wire lately!" Indigo said, twisting the string of her herbal tea bag.

Benjamin took a big sip of his protein smoothie and smacked his lips together, releasing a dramatic exhale. "Ah, that's good." He looked up from his drink and continued. "Listen, Cici's a passionate fireball. I'm not messing with that."

"Well, she *is* messing with our GLO club initiatives. Like the meal riots! Bananas!" Indigo said shaking her head.

"She'd probably have a problem with those too," Sammy smirked.

The GLOs had made great headway on getting the school to add more vegetarian and vegan food options in the school cafeteria. Sammy had even attempted to get Autumn some kosher meals too, once he understood that cashews were not involved. The menu changes had turned out to be a larger fight than they anticipated, primarily because they had run into a forceful opposition to this from the BOTs, and in particular, Cici Bubber.

As Sammy had anticipated, she had joined the BOT club and quickly became a force to be reckoned with. The lunch issue was a particular hot-button issue for Cici, due to her family's employment in the meat industry, as well as their recreational support of hunting. She wanted to get the school *back on track* to support traditional values of the school and the town, and because she had quite a bit of support from other rural kids, she felt a responsibility to be a voice for them on issues that mattered most to students like her.

To protest the proposed new cafeteria menu, she rallied a group of BOT loyalists and launched what she called *Operation Real Food*. There were letters to the principal, lunchtime chants, and a full-blown march through the lunchroom. Her pièce de résistance? Handing out her family's homemade venison bacon to anyone stuck waiting in line for tofu nuggets.

To her *very* vocal disappointment, the school sided with the GLO Club instead — approving "diverse meal options for all." Translation: veggie burgers were here to stay.

Benjamin continued. "Look, she is as passionate about her issues as you are about yours. Don't judge her!"

Indigo gave Benjamin a wounded look that she seemed to know would work immediately.

His head dropped. "Okay, Indy, I'll keep my eye on her."

"Cleo, can you tell us about the BOT...Army, is it?" Indigo gave Cleo a gentle and encouraging smile.

Cleo took a big swig of her water, preparing for her moment in the sun. "Sure Indigo. Um, no actually it is the BOT *Brigade*. So, we..."

Benjamin's hand reached across in front of Cleo as if he was physically holding her back. "Why don't I take this. I know the most about the Brigade that *I* formed."

Sammy was enraged.

He stared at his friend, sulking there in the aftermath of being stifled and silenced, like an afterthought. *WHY does she put up with this?* He toggled between pity for Cleo, rage at Benjamin, and righteousness that she was "getting what she deserved" for betraying him.

Benjamin had noticed how much more momentum the GLO Club had gotten through the creation of the Squad. He decided that he should create a club of leaders to help him do his work too, so that he could go out and work the crowds more forcefully. He didn't see why charisma like his should be wasted on the boring work of paper-pushing or focusing on details.

"Oh sure, go ahead Benjamin, you can describe our BOT movement best." Cleo lowered her head in defeat.

OUR BOT movement. Barf. Sammy's knew his poker face was failing him again.

"The first batch of leaders that we have identified to head up the BOT club's early leadership work are Cici, Louie, Vinnie, and Megan." Benjamin turned. "Oh, and Cleo, of course."

Cici would be heading up her area of expertise — activism.

He had also roped in his two closest soccer teammates, Louie and Vinnie, to serve on the committee. Being that they were the two boys that had harassed Sammy in the bathroom, Cleo's perceived betrayal had gotten so much worse for Sammy with this alignment.

"Louie and Vinnie, what a couple of winners right there." Sammy sat with his arms crossed, sipping his chai and gazing out the floor-to-ceiling coffee shop window, trying hard to mentally escape this conversation by imagining he was already living his intended future dream life in Paris.

"They aren't your biggest fans either, '*Pepper*!'" Benjamin said, making sarcastic air quotes around the nickname.

Sammy sprung up in his seat, ready to rip the lid off his cup and launch his chai over the table into Benjamin's face. "Why don't you just shut the..."

Indigo grabbed Sammy's hand that was holding his drink.

"...he didn't mean anything by it, Sammy. Let's just move on." Indigo was looking worn out from the high wire act of dealing with the warring sides.

"And Megan...as if we don't know what you are planning with that one!" Sammy laughed condescendingly.

"Hey, you have Darla! What's good for the goose is good for the gander!"

The GANDER? How old is this guy?

Megan Yamauchi was Terri's former friend whose falling out had been spurred by the locker debate. Her friendship with Terri had started to crack once they landed on opposite sides of the club war — another Sammy-and-Cleo situation in the making.

Benjamin had intentions of beating the GLOs in every arena — number of members, money raised, impact on school, and most importantly to him, having the most coverage in the school newspaper, the *Prism*.

Truth be told, part of why Benjamin wanted Megan in the leadership is that she was a news writer for the Prism, and he trusted her journalistic ability to dig up dirt. He also had a long-term plan to use her role there to influence the news articles to the favor of the BOTs if necessary. But for now, being a BOT Spy was her assigned role.

"There is no ulterior motive for her involvement. Other than she's smart and committed to the most important club at EHS." Benjamin smiled provokingly.

"You mispronounced *impotent*," Sammy chuckled.

"Okay, okay," Indigo shot a look at Sammy. "Now that all of these pleasantries are out of the way, the real point of this meeting was to discuss the creation of joint meetings between the Squad and Brigade, where the student body can ask us questions and we can present to them each club's new initiatives. Am I summarizing that right, Pep...er...Sammy? You see, Sammy actually brought this idea to me the other day after he and Cleo came up with it."

Benjamin's head snapped over to Cleo with a look of anger and surprise.

A few days ago, Cleo spotted Sammy sitting at their usual lunch table — the one that hadn't felt "usual" in forever. Her heart thudded, but she forced herself forward, tray shaking just a little in her hands.

"Hey," she said, sliding into a seat across from him. "Can we... talk?"

Sammy didn't look up right away. He picked at the crust of his sandwich, calm as ever. "About what?"

She hadn't thought that far ahead. All the big things she'd realized — how she'd hurt him, how she missed him, how Benjamin had gotten between them — tangled together in her head, too heavy to say out loud. So instead, she blurted the safest words she could find.

"Maybe we can just leave the past in the past. Start over?"

Sammy finally looked up. His face was unreadable. "Sure," he said. "No big deal. The past is in the past."

It wasn't the reunion Cleo had pictured, but it was something — a fragile truce, thin as notebook paper.

As part of the truce, they agreed to start a regularly recurring club leaders' meetup, something that might keep future misunderstandings from exploding. It wasn't forgiveness, not really. But for now, it was a start.

Cleo took another sip of water. "Sure, so basically, Sammy and I were talking the other day and came up with the idea to bring the Squad and the Brigade together once a month as a full group. Our working title for this meeting is The Congregation."

"The Congregation? What does that even mean?" Benjamin sulked at being the only one hearing of this plan for the first time.

Cleo smirked to melt his ice a little. "You know, like in church. The congregation is the entire group of people who come to hear a church service, so I figured this was a perfect name for bringing both groups of BOT and GLO leadership together to speak publicly to the rest of the student body. We can also use the time together to strategize joint initiatives for the school that the BOTs and GLOs can collaborate on *together*!"

Sammy cut in, staring darts at Benjamin. "…and it'll be a good way for us to keep our eyes on you guys."

"So, what, basically you want our leaders to get together and speak to the whole school every month? We can brag about the good stuff we've been doing, and recruit new members and stuff?" Benjamin sat up, enticed with the opportunity for increased facetime in front of the school.

"In a nutshell, yes. We were hoping that it would help to keep the clubs aligned in some way, and we can show a united face so that students don't feel that we are at war all the time." Cleo's hands were subconsciously clasped in position of prayer, hoping for a positive outcome.

Benjamin paused momentarily, acting as if there was any further need to convince him. When no one tried, he rendered his verdict.

"I can dig it. How about you, Pepper?"

Sammy sarcastically flashed peace signs, impersonating a 70s hippie. "I can dig it, maaaan…"

"Works for me too!" Indigo smiled. "Okay so what if we do the first meeting of…The Congregation…next week, that way both sides will have a little time to get our presentations in order?"

She knew each club would need time to pull together collections of their accomplishments, as well as laundry lists of missteps that the other club had made. After all, this would be as much a time to brag as it would be to condemn!

"Rock on." Benjamin smiled and sat back in his chair, sipping his smoothie and biting into a cream cheese bagel that he just now remembered he had ordered.

"Oh, one more thing." Cleo paused, seeming hesitant to open a can of worms during a break in the warfare. "Well, so, Ronald asked if he could come to the Congregation meeting. He heard us talking at lunch about it and wants the Compass Club to be represented."

While he only had four total members so far, Ronald felt that they had important viewpoints that should be represented as part of the student body.

"Not a chance!" Benjamin scoffed, spitting some bagel as he spoke.

Indigo joined him, shaking her head. "No way, guys. Come on."

While they agreed about nearly nothing else, Indigo and Benjamin were in alignment about this.

Indigo went first. "If he comes and students hear his centrist every-thing-and-nothing message, the GLOs, and even the BOTs, could lose membership to a club that has no realistic chance of affecting change or doing anything! We just need to limit the options to two. Then students can pick whichever of our clubs is the closest to what they want. One or the other."

Benjamin cut in. "I don't care one iota about losing any BOTs! If anyone is dumb enough to leave the BOTs for *any* other group, I couldn't care less about them. The reason I don't want Ronnie there is because everything he and the Compass Club stands for is ridicu-lous, unrealistic, and a waste of time. Why would we let that dork take away speaking time from us?"

Cleo's hands were clasped tighter than before. She paused, debating if she should argue against the leaders, but this felt too important to stay quiet about. She mustered up her courage and interjected. "I say we let him come. I can't in good conscience tell another club leader that they can't come and represent their followers, just because we are bigger or don't like their message. We should love thy neighbor, and I want everyone to feel they can be heard. And Ronald won't talk too long, I wouldn't worry about that. He will just be happy to be included."

Indigo turned to Sammy. "What do you think?"

Sammy maintained his slumped and dismissive posture, while he disguised pouting as aloofness.

"Let him come. I mean really, *how* could you feel threatened by *Ronald*?" Sammy said dismissively.

His implication of weakness lit Benjamin like a match. "Fine, let the idiot come. How much damage could one kid do anyway?"

INDIGO

"¡Mamá! ¡Vamos!" Indigo impatiently twisted one of the feathers in her hair as she waited for her mother, Mercedes, to come down the stairs. As always, Indigo's house was a whirl of action as her four little siblings rushed around the room, playing, chasing, crying, laughing, screaming, and fighting.

Indigo was the oldest of the group by far, so she often served as a second mother to her little siblings.

"Despacito Ruby..." she said, as one of her little sisters rolled by on a skateboard.

"¡Vale Indy!" Ruby's squeaky voice responded.

"¿En Inglés?" Indigo quizzed.

"Okay Indeee! I'll slow down!" Ruby chirped as she continued on by.

All five of the children had the same mother and father, at least in terms of love. Indigo's biological father had left her mother, Mercedes, soon after Indigo was born. Throughout her young life, she hardly had any interaction with him other than message-less greeting cards she received on her birthdays. Aside from this, Indigo's only connection to him was her last name, Ortiz.

Mercedes's husband, Dante de la Iglesia, wasn't just the biological father of Indigo's four siblings — he was the only dad Indigo had ever really known. In Emerald, everyone knew Dante as the local politician who dreamed of becoming mayor, not for power but because he was obsessed with making life better for their town and the rural communities around it. He showed up everywhere — church basements, school gyms, town hall steps — speaking up for any person or group that needs a helping hand or the world overlooks. His biggest fight was against the opioid crisis that stole too many neighbors.

It didn't pay much, but the mission and impact he made on the community he loved was all the compensation he needed. Indigo adored him and quietly hoped that one day people would talk about her with the same kind of fierce respect that they did about him.

In addition to the five children and their parents, Indigo's grandmother lived with the family as well. Her name was Dorotea, but everyone just called her "Abuela."

As Indigo stood there at the front door tapping her foot impatiently, above the chaos a raspy voice rose above the children's noise. "¡Basta!"

Indigo saw Abuela dodging children as she tried with one hand to navigate her walker around their toys all over the hallway floor. Her other hand grumpily waved over her head, attempting to protect herself from any rogue ball or toy carelessly thrown at her.

She spoke under her breath, complaining to no one in particular. ¡Dios mío, esto parece una guardería! Mejor me voy a la morgue unos años antes, total, ya casi me toca. Allá por lo menos hay silencio."

Indigo burst into laughter. "Abuela! You aren't ready for the morgue! And I don't think you need to move there to get rest. I know this feels like a daycare sometimes, but before you know it, all these cuties will be grown and gone. Then how will you feel about all the years that you spent being so grumpy about them?" She gently touched Abuela's shoulder and smirked, bracing herself for a hilarious response.

"I'll tell you how I'll feel when they are grown up...DEAD!" she said with a comedic cranky tone. She continued, not missing a beat.

"Forget the little perritos, how are you, my beauty?" She reached her aged and gnarled tan hand up to grab a piece of Indigo's hair and lovingly twisted it in her wrinkled fingers. Even though it had never been specifically said, Indigo had always gleaned that she was Abuela's favorite.

"I'm fine, Abuela."

"Are you still dating that big dopey boy, Ben-ha-min?"

"No Abuela, I broke up with him a while ago. We just didn't see life in the same way, I guess." She looked at the floor with a bit of defeat, worried that her family would be disappointed in her for breaking up with a rich and popular kid like Benjamin.

"That's good! He was pretty, but wasn't very bright, that one. I don't think his elevator goes all the way to the top floor anyway. ¿Me entiendes?" She giggled and put her little hand over her mouth.

Indigo smiled, relieved that turning down what seemed like a prized relationship to many hadn't disappointed her family. "¡Sí Abuela! Lo sé."

While she often found herself missing him, Indigo regularly had to remind herself that there was no way she could reconcile with Benjamin.

He was a simpleton, she told herself.

He was emotionally immature, she told herself.

He was not in her mental league, she told herself.

And yet...

Indigo began twisting one of the dozen or so bracelets on her wrist, a blue beaded one with a silver heart charm attached to it. Engraved on the charm were the letters "IR." Benjamin had given her this bracelet back when they were dating, and the letters stood for Indigo Rosa...what he declared her married name would be when they tied the knot someday.

While she appreciated the gesture, this bracelet was an example of the complete lack of understanding that Benjamin had of what

Indigo wanted in life, and a symbol of everything that was wrong with their relationship.

Indigo had always been clear about one thing: she wasn't the type of person to change her name for a man. Other women could make whatever choices felt right for them, but she carried her Latina identity like a banner, unshakable and untouchable. Marriage wasn't on her radar — never had been, never would be.

Probably.

Either way, Benjamin definitely wasn't the person who would change that. She continued looking down at the bracelet, twisting it in a daydream.

Or was he?

Suddenly, Mercedes came rushing down the stairs, simultaneously twisting a scarf around her neck and putting on earrings. "Soy lista! Let's go Indy!"

Indigo helped Abuela into her favorite rocking chair, tucked her under her blanket and handed her the remote control, kissed her grandmother on the cheek, and rushed out the door with her mom.

As they walked to the car, a voice bellowed from the upstairs bathroom window. "¡Adiós mis amores!" Dante shouted out the window at his girls, like he did every day without fail.

"¡Adiós papá!" Indigo shouted.

Indigo's mother blew him a kiss as they both dove into the car.

Today was a big day — the first meeting of the Congregation. Indigo could already feel her stomach twisting. She was leading the whole thing — the biggest, loudest, most opinionated mix of students the school had to offer — and she had no idea what Sammy was planning to do.

That part scared her the most.

Since their last talk, he'd been buried in GLO business. Every time she saw him, he was taping up flyers, printing posters, or fiddling with some shiny new buttons. When she asked what he was up to, he'd just grin and sarcastically say, "Nothing for you to worry about, *Madame President*." Which, of course, made her worry even more.

It was starting to feel like *his* club now. Sammy's "Squad" was quietly taking over the GLO Club, running meetings and making decisions while Indigo was left smiling onstage, trying to sound like she knew what was going on.

Not that she didn't appreciate their help — organization had never exactly been her superpower. Details, schedules, sign-up sheets? No thanks. Indigo was a big-picture person, a speaker, a motivator. She loved the spark of standing in front of a crowd and making them believe in something.

But lately, she'd been doing that for causes she hadn't even heard of until the moment she stepped up to the podium. She didn't mind being the face of change — she just wished she actually knew what she was selling before she had to sell it. She knew she needed to find time to talk to Sammy prior to the meeting at recess. She had to find out what in the world he had planned for her to do while she was onstage during the Congregation today.

She only hoped she agreed with his plans.

"Today's a big day, Indy! You are just like your Papá, always focusing on changing the world! We are both *so* proud of you." Mercedes stole a glance of her daughter as she drove her to school. Mercedes's dark eyes and beautiful smile were bursting with pride at the thought of her daughter's achievements. "Are you ready for today?"

"Más o menos," Indigo said, with a hint of reservation.

"What's wrong, mí amor?"

"Oh nothing, I guess I'm just nervous. I don't know what Sammy has planned for today, so that always has me a little on edge." Indigo fiddled with the feathers in her hair again.

"He sounds like a good boy, so I'm sure everything will be fine." Mercedes was a big fan of what she knew of Sammy. Sassy, funny, strong…what's not to love?

"Yeah, I'm sure it will," Indigo said, unconvinced.

"And look at you! You look so preeetttyyy!" Mercedes said, twisting Indigo's hair with one hand, while the other continued to steer the car. "Speaking of pretty, what do you think Sammy will wear today?" she said with a giddy chuckle. "I can't wait to meet this kid in person, he sounds *maravilloso*!"

"Oh, you'd love him mom. He's a really cool kid. He's quirky, but that's what I love about him. He gets picked on sometimes by jerks like Benny, but he doesn't give a d...."

"Indy! Language!" Mercedes scolded. Her face quickly softened. "I'm glad he stands up to Benny. That kid needs to be put in his place. He is *way* too conservative for a young man. He should let loose a little! He needs menos Biblia y más *baile*!"

"You wouldn't say that if you saw how bad his dancing is," Indigo said.

Mercedes persisted with her nosiness. "Why don't you date Sammy yourself?"

"Well...uh...I'm not sure I'm his type. Plus, he's younger. I need a sophisticated older man!" She instinctively covered up Benjamin's bracelet, somehow hoping to convince herself he was not part of her love equation.

"Ay, ay, ay, Indy..." her mother shuddered at the thought of Indy with an older student. She wanted to keep her as innocent as possible, for as long as possible.

The car pulled up to the school, and they entered the parental drop-off line. Three cars ahead of them, Indigo noticed Sammy and Cleo getting out of Alex's Tesla. She strained to lean up far enough to try to snoop at what Sammy was carrying.

"Newspapers?" she accidentally said out loud.

"What?" her mother said.

"See that white car up there? That brown haired boy is Sammy. Can you tell what that pile of papers is that Sammy is carrying?"

Mercedes rolled down her window and stuck her head out of the window to try to see better.

"¡Mamá! You are so embarrassing!" Indigo dropped her head and hid.

"Tranquila, girl." She continued to examine Sammy's movements. "I love his little cartera!" she said. "And those sneakers… ooohhhh!!!…" She snapped her fingers as applause.

"Focus! What is he carrying?" Indigo was losing patience with her mother, while also trying to get a jump start on what Sammy was up to.

"Sí, those are newspapers. A big stack of them. I wonder what he has planned!" Mercedes was bursting with curiosity and excitement. "Can parents come to this Congregation today? I'm dying to see this for myself!"

Newspapers? Indigo's mind rushed with possibilities, good and bad. She pondered the best- and worst-case possibilities as her mother inched up in line.

"Indy! Get going, people are waiting!" Indigo looked up to see herself at the front of the line. "Oh sorry. ¡Té amo mamá!" She leapt out of the car.

As she rushed into the school, she felt a hand on her shoulder. She turned around and saw the last person she wanted to see today.

PRISM

"Oh, hey Ronald, what's up?" Indigo said through a forced smile.

"Hey Indigo! Looking forward to the Congregation meeting today? I know I am!" said Ronald, with a little extra bounce to his step today.

"Sure am," she said distantly, her eyes darting around the hallway in pursuit of Sammy.

"Thanks again for letting me come. I think that it is really important that the views of the Compass Club be heard. We want to represent not only the members of our club, but also *any* student at EHS, even if they aren't part of a club at all. I think we will be a good influence on everyone, because we can help everyone find common ground and find a happy medium to all the silly arguments that bog everyone down…"

"Sure…compromise, middle ground, holding hands, kumbaya, all that good stuff. Listen, I need to run Ronald. See you at recess," Indigo said dismissively. She dashed away down the hall, making a beeline to Sammy's locker.

Sammy had just approached and was fumbling with his pile of newspapers while attempting to unlock his locker combination. Just then, Indigo arrived. He didn't even have to lift his head to know she was there, as her light floral perfume always announced her presence prior to any visual confirmation.

"Hey Indy, what's up?"

"What's with the newspapers?" she said inquisitively.

"Take a look," Sammy said cryptically, flashing a mischievous smile.

"How did you get these?" Indigo asked as she reached for one.

"Darla gave me an early batch. Just read!" Sammy said impatiently.

Indigo picked up one of the newspapers and looked at the front page. Right under the school paper's Prism title and logo, she saw the headline:

GLO Club Fights to Keep Kindness Alive at EHS

By Darla DiAngi

A huge smile spread across Indigo's face. She couldn't wait to sink her teeth into this.

Times are changing here at Emerald High School (EHS) school. The days of being bullied into following outdated rules of the past are over. With the creation of the GLO Club by Sammy Iris and his team of fellow students, all EHS students now have the chance to join a club that cares about them.

The club began when Sammy and another student wanted to fight back against the terrible events that occurred on the day that will be remembered forever, the Great "Locker Assault." Sadly, Sammy was one of the students who was a victim of the BOT Club's vicious attack on freedom here at EHS. Like they did to so many other students, the BOTs damaged and destroyed Sammy's personal items as part of their plan to take away our freedoms, and to force us all to obey their limiting and oppressive rules.

Instead of stooping to their level, Sammy decided to start a club that would take the high road. The club focuses on charity work, giving back, and standing up for those who need our help. The GLO Club, which stands for Goodness, Love, and Opportunity, is now accepting new members.

Today at recess there will be a meeting of the Congregation, a peaceful get-together with all GLO, BOT, and other interested students in attendance. In addition to Sammy Iris, speakers will include Indigo Ortiz and Benjamin

Rosa. The meeting will be held next to the rock wall. To register to become a GLO kid, please see GLO Director, Sammy Iris.

To the right of the article was a large photo of Sammy standing next to his plain, undecorated locker, holding a sad pile of wreckage including his framed Harry Styles Vogue cover with the glass broken, his crumpled Theo and Gwen poster, and his photo with Cleo. His face was hanging with an over exaggerated sad, solemn expression, and his large dark eyes looked pitifully into the camera. Below the photo, the caption reads:

Damage from the BOTs is everywhere
Photo credit: Matthew Bailey

Indigo stared at the newspaper long after she had finished reading the article. She was trying to decide how best to respond without picking a fight.

Sammy seemed irritated by her delay in congratulating him on what he saw as this victory. "You know it isn't easy to get this kind of press! This is fantastic for the GLOs. You're WELCOME!" he snipped.

In fact, Sammy did have to put in a great deal of effort to get this piece published. While the reporter, Darla, was a supporter of the GLO mission, she had intentionally not joined the club due to her need to remain neutral to honor her "journalistic ethics." Sammy had worked very hard to convince her to write the article about the GLO Club and even had to promise her fee-free entrance into any of the club events if she ever decided to come or join in the future. Giving her a small benefit like that seemed to be a small price to pay to get this sort of press.

Indigo looked up slowly from the paper and broke her silence. "'GLO Club was started by Sammy and another student? Speakers include Indigo and Benjamin?' What is going on here?"

"What?" Sammy said innocently. "What part of that isn't true?"

"Sammy!" Indigo exclaimed, letting her frustration slip out more than she intended. "I came to you with the idea to start the GLO Club. I am the President of the club, and I am not even mentioned except as a speaker? How would anyone know I was even involved in starting this by reading this article?"

"Is that why you are doing this, for the recognition? Indigo, we are doing this to change lives. I didn't realize it was a popularity contest for you!" Sammy paused, looking proud to let his message sink in. "Next time I will be sure your name is flashed everywhere so you get the proper attention." He overdramatically rolled his eyes to put a cherry on his judgmental cake.

"Give me a break, Pep! First of all, you clearly did think it was a popularity contest, as you made sure you were mentioned in there over and over again, not to mention *that photo*!" she laughed judgmentally.

"What's wrong with that photo?" Sammy said, fuming.

"I know for a fact that your Harry Styles frame did not have any broken glass from the Locker Assault, because I saw it just last week in perfect condition. Remember on Friday, when you were showing off how you had modeled your hair off his Vogue cover? Did you break that glass to make the BOTs look worse, and for you to come off as more pathetic?"

"PATHETIC?" Sammy was enraged now. "How dare you call me pathetic! If you had any idea how much work it took for me to get an article WITH A PICTURE published in the paper that showed the true evils of the BOTs, and how the GLOs are the answers to the students' prayers, you would be on your knees thanking me! Instead, you just complain and make it about yourself. Unbelievable."

Indigo started to feel sorry for her actions, then she paused. She had conceived of the idea of the GLO Club, had named the club herself, had co-founded the club that she was now the President of, and yet she was being called self-centered for wanting to be mentioned as more than a speaker at a meeting.

On the other hand, Sammy had been credited as the founder, Director, and the worst victim of the Locker Assault.

How was she in the wrong again?

She knew better than to argue with him, however. She quickly backed down for pragmatic reasons.

"Look, it's a good article, actually a great one. Thank you for your work to get it in the paper. It makes the club look amazing, and certainly does that for *you* too," she said sharply. "Next time, maybe you could mention my involvement, though, as I want to inspire other women of color to get involved in leadership. Okay?"

"Sure, whatever." Sammy sulked as he slammed the stack of papers into the locker and closed it hurriedly as he rushed to class.

"Wait, Sammy!" Indigo rushed after him. "What am I saying at the meeting? I know you have been working on lots of things for the Congregation today. What topics do you want me to touch on?"

He opened his notebook as they walked. He ripped out two pages from his notebook and waved them in her face. "Well, I had prepared a speech for you, but maybe I should let you write your own, since you are the big boss and I'm just a flunky helper!"

"Pep, you know that's not it. I was just caught off guard at how often you were mentioned..." she paused, realizing she wasn't headed in a direction that would get her where she needed to go. "I'm sorry, you're right. I'd be so appreciative if I could read the speech that you wrote, if you would be kind enough to share it."

Sammy stood there with his arms crossed, tapping his rainbow striped foot. "Could you write your own speech if you had to? Do you even *know* what your own club stands for?"

Indigo looked around, embarrassed at this public and unflattering conflict within the GLO leadership right before the

Congregation. Sammy was getting louder and more animated with each response.

"Of course, I could, Sammy. But you know the issues the best and are the strongest communicator…as we saw in the original GLO meeting," she chucked self-deprecatingly.

"You can say that again," he said. "I've got to go. Do what you want with it." He tossed the pages on the ground and left.

Indigo dodged and weaved between the passerby students as she attempted to pick up the speech pages, almost getting her hand stepped on twice. She finally snatched up the pages from the floor, which now had muddy footprints all over them. She started reading the speech.

Dang. It's amazing.

THE CONGREGATION

As he headed out to recess, Sammy was a mix of emotions. The tiff with Indigo earlier had left a sour taste in his mouth and sent him into the Congregation meeting feeling unappreciated and bitter. However, at this point he had decided for practicality's sake to aim all his frustration toward Benjamin and the BOTs.

He arrived at the rock wall to find Indigo the first one there, feverishly studying her speech and trying to commit as much of it as possible to memory. She looked up eagerly.

"Hey Pep! I'm so glad you're here. Let's run over everything now if we can, before Benny and Cleo get here." Indigo was focused like Sammy had never seen her before.

While he was still aggravated with Indigo, considering the limited time, Sammy decided to put aside his theatrics and emotions for the good of the GLOs.

"Okay so here's what I was thinking. I was thinking that since Benjamin won the coin toss and is speaking first, during his speech I would walk around and hand out copies of the Prism papers to all the students to distract everyone from his message. They will be paying zero attention to him and just reading about me...I mean us. The GLOs. You know what I mean..." he stammered, trying to fix his slip up. "Then, when you go to speak, everyone will be excited to hear from you since the article does such a great job of promoting *us*!"

Indigo looked concerned. "That is a great idea, but it seems sort of impolite, doesn't it? I mean, I don't want to take away his ability to speak to the students who like him."

"Oh, please," Sammy rolled his eyes. "We aren't here to help the BOTs or their roBOT followers. We are here to help the GLOs. Period."

"But we got into this to make sure that all students had a voice. I'm just worried if we now only make moves that help our side, that we are no better than Benny." Indigo twisted her hair feathers, as she always did when she was nervous.

"That's how you get ahead, girlfriend. Wake up." Sammy nonchalantly unpacked his bag, which was full of items for the meeting. Sign-up sheets, pens, Prism newspapers, buttons, and his big surprise...glow sticks!

He snapped one in the middle, activating the glowing light, and waved it in Indigo's face.

"Could you love it more? *Glow* sticks for the GLO kids! Because we are the warm GLO in the BOT darkness. Get it?" He gazed down at his neon yellow glowing stick with pride.

"Sure, that'll be fun!" Indigo said distractedly, as she looked down at her papers. "Now about this speech..."

"Crap, here come Benjamin and Cleo." Sammy crossed his arms, subconsciously communicating his contempt for them.

Benjamin walked with an air of authority like Sammy had never seen. He had neatly combed his usually wild hat-headed hair and was wearing a pair of dress pants with a button up shirt.

Red, of course.

Cleo trailed behind, fumbling with boxes and papers as usual. She too had on red — a lovely little short-sleeved dress with a white scalloped collar. Sammy had never seen this dress before, but he hated to admit to himself that he thought she looked amazing. He thought the same about Benjamin too. Sammy was begrudgingly impressed with how professional and organized the BOTs appeared to be for the Congregation.

He glanced over at Indigo, examining her flowy bohemian frock, and for a minute he wished that she had shown up in a more formal and polished way. He then looked down at his own clothes: elastic fake leather pants, a T-shirt with the overhead city map of Paris on it, and of course, the rainbow shoes.

He pondered if they should have stepped up their game a little. He was feeling very insecure now, just moments after he was full of confidence.

Then he shook himself out of it. Please. He was *Sammy Iris.* No one out-fashions him. The GLOs weren't about status or dress clothes — they were for everyone, period. If the country club crew wanted to show up looking like they were headed to a debutante ball, that was their mistake. Good luck connecting with the rest of the students now.

"Hey guys," Cleo said cheerfully as she approached. She dropped the famous BOT supply box on the rock wall next to Sammy's. Benjamin grunted something that sounded like "what's up" as he sauntered by. Cleo continued, trying to break the ice. "This'll be fun!"

"It sure will!" A new voice entered the conversation. Everyone turned and saw Ronald walking up. He was wearing a jacket and tie, the most formal of anyone, with a briefcase in his hand and a committed look in his eye.

Sammy and Cleo greeted Ronald, while a displeased Indigo and Benjamin feigned busy. Sammy looked over and saw Indigo and Benjamin chatting to one another, laughing, pushing each other, and finding any excuse to make physical contact. This concerned Sammy, but this was drama for another day.

"What order are we speaking in today? Does anyone have a schedule?" Ronald asked. "Because if not, I prepared something..." he said, reaching into his briefcase.

"Thank you, no," Sammy said, dismissively waving off Ronald. "I've got everything planned out here."

He handed agendas to Indigo, Benjamin, Cleo, and Ronald, and kept one himself. In patented Sammy-fashion, the light purple paper that the agenda was printed on was also bubblegum-scented, which he claimed added "personality" to whatever was printed on it.

The agenda read:

SCHEDULE
- *The Meeting of the Great Congregation*
- *Welcome*
- *Introduction by Sammy Iris*
- *Speech by Benjamin Rosa from the BOT Club*
- *Speech by Indigo Ortiz from the GLO Club*
- *(If time permits) A few words from Ronald Ross from the Compass Club*
- *Closing statement by Sammy Iris*
- *Questions and GLO Club Signups with Sammy Iris*

As everyone was reading the agenda, students began to gather around them. The Congregation was about to start. While he had seen Indigo's posturing on top of the rock wall as a pompous move last time, Sammy had changed his tune due to the sheer number of students coming over. He decided to step up on the rock wall to be better seen for his introductions and welcome.

He looked around at the leaders who were still making their way through reading the schedule, and he leaned down whispering "Good? Everything good?" as he made a thumbs up gesture in anticipation of their seamless acceptance of his plans.

"Greetings EHS students!" Sammy said with a theatrical flair of his hand over his head. The crowd clapped and laughed.

Without notes and only from memory, he launched into a dramatic, lengthy speech fit for a king, or more applicably here, a speech fit for a President of a Club. But of course, *Indigo* was his President, he was the Director. The fact that there was little true distinction between those titles had not been well thought out, at least by Indigo. Sammy's intentionality was paying off, and he loved that the titles were perceived with nearly equal respect.

Sammy spoke of the struggles and strife at the school, he spoke of a recent "dark period" that the school had endured, and while he didn't directly mention the BOTs by name, he was as intentionally obvious as possible. He lamented the way that the student body had been led off track by some unnamed evil forces, but thankfully there was a new and inclusive club, who also remained nameless in the speech, that was developed to fight for peace and love at EHS.

With the passion and moral superiority that he brought to his words, it felt impossible to make an argument against him or the GLO Club. Even those that didn't agree with him or the GLOs felt helpless to say so, for fear of being seen as monsters. He handled the crowd, and the message, like a master orator.

"And now for our first speaker. I'd like to welcome up Boz..." he slapped his forehead in embarrassment, hoping the snafu went unnoticed. "Benjamin Rosa from the BOT Club."

Half of the crowd clapped while the other half stood silent in defiance.

"Hey guys," Benjamin said nervously, shuffling his papers in front of him. While he was used to being an authority wherever he went, he clearly was not feeling comfortable speaking formally to a group this large.

Sammy saw that the papers he was fidgeting with were not a speech at all, but a list of accomplishments that he had prepared to brag about.

Sammy was both amused and worried for Benjamin, as it seemed that he planned to improv a speech on the spot in front of this many people.

At first, Benjamin rambled a lot and got off track more times than he was on track.

Ironic for the leader of the "Back on Track" Club. Sammy was holding back laughter.

But Benjamin did possess the undeniably important, yet intangible and untrainable quality of charisma. When he spoke, whether they loved or hated him, people were compelled to listen.

He spoke about how the school had started to lack morals due to so many years of lax behavior being permitted. He talked about how the student body needed a true leader, a job that could only be done successfully by him, and him alone.

From the crumpled pieces of paper he was clutching, he rattled off a disjointed list of accomplishments achieved by the BOTs and, according to him, attributable primarily to himself alone.

He never mentioned any of his BOT members or Brigade leaders, not even sweet worker-bee Cleo, who stood there, overlooked and underappreciated. Again.

After a couple of minutes, Sammy got up in the middle of Benjamin's speech and grabbed the pile of Prism newspapers. He started passing them out to the student onlookers in the crowd, pointing to the cover article each time he handed one out. If students began to speak to him to ask a question or make a statement, he made a theatrically big but ingenuine "shh" motion in front of his mouth to appease the BOT onlookers, then continued to intentionally speak at normal volume to engage the student.

Several students offered Sammy a back pat or a hug of condolence when they saw his pitiable photo on the newspaper cover. He accepted the sympathy and attention gleefully.

The centerpiece of Benjamin's rambling improv was a series of insults aimed at the GLO Club, both as a whole and at Indigo directly. "Can you *believe* how much time and money the GLOs spent in supporting the refugee center? What do we have, one refugee family here? The priority of any club should be to serve the largest majority of kids, not just tiny fringe groups!"

A few claps were heard. "And wasting time and money promoting these 'hippy-dippy' meal plans like vegetarianism and kosher meals are hurting the hard-working local meat industry families like Cici's, and yours..." he said pointing out at the crowd, hoping to bring them into the victim pool and attaching them to his cause.

He spoke against the GLO Club's lax policies regarding dress, decorum, social behavior. Sammy kept glancing at his watch, cognizant that time was running short. He looked over at Indigo who pointed at her wrist and made a motion for Benjamin to wrap it up. Sammy made several attempts to subtly signal to Benjamin that his time was limited, but it was clear that he had no intention of allowing another speaker to be heard.

After another minute or two, Sammy walked up and started clapping, encouraging the crowd to do so as well, to force Benjamin to step away and surrender the spotlight.

"...and this is why you must join the BOTs. If you aren't a BOT, you might as well be nothing!" he said to complete his speech.

What an inspirational rally cry, Sammy thought scathingly.

As Sammy rushed up to introduce Indigo, Cleo darted in front of him, looking nervous but determined.

"Hey guys! I also just wanted to say that the BOTs stand for much more than just being tough. We aren't against freedoms; we just want to be sure that tradition isn't lost in this modern world. Things like church or God are often forgotten, and we want to be sure there is a place for students who still want those things in their lives! We don't want to be forgotten either. Why, just this week at my church group..."

"Thank you!" Sammy said while clapping, ushering her off the wall. Cleo stumbled as she was strong-armed off the rocks. Her speech conveyed sentiments that were much more eloquent and positive than Benjamin's, so Sammy had no choice but to shut her down before she started to garner even more momentum for the BOTs.

It was too late. About half of the crowd clapped excitedly in support of the BOT message. Sammy had underestimated the popularity of their platform. He took this as a challenge.

He pushed forward with the agenda. "We are short on time here, so I don't want to waste a moment. Please welcome the one, the only, Indigo Ortiz from the GLO Club!"

Indigo took the stage like a bohemian forest fairy, full of buoyance and charm and sprite-like effervescence in everything she said.

"First of all, I just have to respond to something that was said earlier. I cannot *believe* that anyone would criticize the GLO kids for helping the so-called 'fringe-groups.' America is built on helping one another, no matter if it is a few or many. We as the GLOs are committed to using our power and influence to help those who need it the most. It is time for the school to remove any obedience to dusty old values still in practice and start living in the modern world with enlightened views!"

Sammy stood on the side of the wall, encouraging the crowd to clap at any of the dramatic pauses that he had built into the speech.

Indigo continued, conforming to Sammy's ideal delivery of his written words as if they were her own, effortlessly sharing the message from memory with passion and conviction.

She spoke of a future filled with hope, peace, and love for all students.

Sammy stood there with pride as his melodic words rang out across the school yard — delivered by Indigo — gracing everyone who heard his message. Just then, he heard her reaching the end of the speech.

"And so, I ask that you all consider joining our movement towards Goodness, Love, and Opportunity by becoming a GLO kid. To help you glow a little bit brighter starting right now..." she turned and motioned to Sammy. "…let's GLO together!" she giggled. Sammy reached into his backpack and began throwing out glow sticks into the crowd. Everyone was laughing and squealing with delight as they scrambled to get their hands on one.

Benjamin and Cleo looked on enviously, wishing they had come up with a gimmick to reel in more registrants.

As the laughter and chaos started to minimize, Sammy walked back up on the wall. Ronald flattened his tie and buttoned his coat, making sure he was as prepared as possible when Sammy made his introductions.

"I want to thank everyone for coming out today. Please see me if you'd like to sign up for the GLO Club. You can catch me anytime in the hallway at my fabulous locker, which WILL be brought back to life this week."

He shot a sassy look over at Benjamin and Cleo. "And now…" he paused.

Ronald stood up and began walking to the wall.

"It seems we are out of time as recess is nearly over. Thank you for coming, and we will see you next time!" He smiled just as the bell rang, beckoning the students back into the school. The crowd was laughing and chirping with joy as they headed back with their pink and green and blue and yellow and orange glow sticks illuminating the cloudy day.

Sammy high-fived Indigo and began collecting supplies and stray glow sticks. Ronald came rushing over.

"What was *that*? I have as much right to be heard as you all do! The Compass Club represents lots of kids, and I think if they could hear my message today, they may have preferred us to *either* of you!"

"Look, Ronald, there just wasn't time. I put on the schedule 'if time allows' for your portion and, well, time didn't allow. It's probably best if they pick either the GLOs or the BOTs anyway, because you don't really have a chance next to us!" Sammy said glibly.

"I don't stand a chance if I'm not even allowed to be heard! How will they even know that our club is an option?" Ronald said angrily.

"Come on Ronnie," Benjamin said, patting him so firmly on the back that he fell forward. "You never stood a chance on your own anyway. Just pick a side and get on board with the program."

Everyone gathered their items and began walking back into the school. Benjamin cracked open his copy of the Prism with the prominent GLO article that everyone had been examining during his speech. As he attempted to walk and read at the same time, he began tripping over curbs and rocks, his smile fading and his brow furrowing with each unflattering paragraph he read.

As they started walking away, Sammy and Indigo were chirping like two canaries at how successful they felt their show had been. Cleo looked back over her shoulder as she trailed behind Benjamin carrying her large boxes, giving Ronald a little smile of apology.

Ronald stood there, his presence dismissed, and his viewpoints discarded. He understood that the other clubs were bigger, and more well known, and had more power. But he also knew that his compromise stances would appeal, at least in part, to most students in some way.

He picked up his briefcase, loosened his tie by tugging at the knot, and walked into the school, defeated, but not deterred.

THE SWARM

"I'm sorry. I can't. It just doesn't feel right to do that," Megan Yamauchi said hesitantly. "I can't just make up stories and say they are true. I take my job as a writer very seriously." She continued quietly eating her lunch, surrounded by BOTs as she sat in the cafeteria's Red Sea.

Cleo winced inwardly at the bait and switch happening. She had been the one to invite Megan to lunch, and from the way things were going, it probably felt like a trap to her — Cleo hadn't even spoken since Megan showed up. This was clearly The Benjamin Show.

"Look, those GLO twits have been churning out news in the Prism about their club week after week. Darla is basically Sammy's puppet, writing anything he wants her to in those articles. Actually, the Prism as a *whole* seems to be a GLO puppet. I need to get the BOTs in the news, and FAST!" Benjamin was insistent.

"Do you know how hard it was to get this job at the Prism? I want to be a journalist when I grow up, so I need to do a good job." Megan paused. "I don't even totally understand…what are you asking me to do?"

It was clear that Megan's resistance was breaking down. Cleo leaned up, hoping to create some clarity here. "We wanted to discuss how we can get a more well-rounded picture of the BOTs in the newspaper. Our goals of keeping some traditional values at school are getting mixed up as some sort of attempt at eliminating freedoms. We want to do good things too! For example, some of our next plans are to start a "Letters to the Troops" campaign, do a clothing drive for the veterans, and host an entrepreneur workshop for future business leaders…"

Benjamin cut in, as if Cleo wasn't speaking at all. "Megan, I'm not asking you to break any rules. I just want you to block the GLOs from getting articles in the paper for the next few weeks and put in some good ones for us. That's not asking too much considering that your paper is a billboard for them! So, I'm thinking…" Benjamin paused and folded his hands, putting his index fingers under his chin in thought, "something like 'EHS is *Finally* Back on Track since Benjamin Rosa Moved to Town.'" He waved his hand in front of him as if he was envisioning it on a movie theater marquis. "Wouldn't that be great?" he smiled, attempting to convince her with contagious enthusiasm.

"Do you want me to feature the BOTs, or *you*? Maybe I could write something more about the club, like featuring how you guys did that 'say no to drugs' digital campaign? That was cool! Or all of the plans that Cleo just shared, that is good stuff," Megan tried valiantly to keep the discussion on the rails.

Benjamin was reluctant. "Mmm, yeah, but I really think if we focus on how things have changed since *I've* gotten here, people will want to follow me. After all, the BOTs couldn't exist without *me*."

Cleo furrowed her brow. "Benjamin, I'm not sure that this is entirely true…"

He continued without skipping a beat. "Yes, yes, I am sure, I need to keep the kids focused on me. Maybe I won't be a BOT forever, who knows? They are lucky to have me — if they don't keep me happy maybe I'll break off and create something even better!" He looked at her with a look of surprise. "Get this — if you can believe it, some BOT kids were talking about joining the GLO kids down at the Country Club in their protest of the gas guzzling cars of

the members that are apparently *so* 'environmentally unfriendly.'"
He flashed air quotes with his fingers, using a mocking voice when
speaking the words. "There's no way I'd join in on that! Everyone in
the Rosa family is members at that club!"

He was emphatic about the focus of her article. "No, we need to
keep things simple, keep the kids listening to me. I will lead them
on the right path, get everything on track."

"So...are you saying you *have* gotten the school Back on Track
and that we need to *keep* it on track, or that it *isn't* back on track yet
and we need you to get there?" Megan asked inquisitively. She had
taken out her notebook and had begun taking notes.

"We needed to get back on track, and now that I am at EHS, we
are back on track. Now we need to *stay* on track, or we will *fall* off
track, and then we will need to get back on track *again*. Get it?"
Even Benjamin looked a little confused.

Cleo was getting worried. This conversation was definitely not
on track.

"Ohhhkkaayy..." Megan continued absently speaking as she
made notes. She finished and looked up at him. "So, here's the thing.
I cannot keep the GLO articles out of the Prism. I just can't. It is a
free press. However, I can get a few articles about the BOTs in there.
If I were you, I'd go home and sleep on it before you choose to make
every article about you. This is about your *movement*, not just you,
right?" she asked with genuine curiosity.

"It's about us. And who is the best to lead us? Me! Benjamin Rosa.
Certainly not that incense-burning hippie Latina, or even worse,
Sammy the Rainbow Chaser," he snickered.

He paused after that comment, a slight pang of guilt building
up in his stomach. He'd never admit it, but he admired Sammy's
boldness and liked Indigo's free spiritedness...okay, he liked nearly
everything about *her*. But as his dad Wyatt always said, strength is
what makes winners!

Bow wow wow.

Megan continued to scribble. "Okay, here's what I'm willing to do. I will agree to run the first article as a feature on you and the BOTs, but can you please send me that list of accomplishments that you read in the speech yesterday? I also plan to use some of the information and quotes that you and Cleo said today, but I'll of course remove things like the 'rainbow chaser' or the 'incense-burning' insults..."

Benjamin cut her off. "No! Keep that in there. Kids will love that. They like a straight shooter." He forced a smug smile — the perfect look for "Alpha Benjamin," the persona he felt obligated to maintain.

Megan tried to hide her shock. "Wow, okay. Are you sure?"

Benjamin nodded.

Cleo protested. "No, there's no way we are calling Sammy a rainbow..."

"Don't you have to set up for that BOT recruitment event? You better get going." Benjamin smiled and waved Cleo away. She reluctantly got up to leave, realizing there was no reason for her to waste her time here anyway.

Megan continued. "I'll run with it then. You should see a feature in next week's edition. I have no idea if the GLO kids have another article in there as well, so don't ask me."

"If they do have one, put it on page three or something. They've had enough attention. It's *my* time now!" Benjamin grabbed Megan's still scribbling hand, shook it in appreciation, and started to leave the table in triumph.

Then, he turned around, came back, and leaned down to whisper something in her ear. "Make sure to wear red to school from now on, okay? Out of respect, you get it," he said, nodding.

He stood up and began to walk away. As he left, Megan noticed the Red Sea quickly disappearing from the lunchroom, following behind Benjamin like a swarm of bees. A more fascinating sight she had never seen.

She continued scribbling in her notebook well past the time that her ending lunch bell had rung. This interaction, this potential piece of news was so different from anything that the Prism or even EHS as a whole had ever seen, that it was just too good to pass up.

Class would have to wait.

Rainbow Chaser

"'*Rainbow chaser?*' What does that even mean?" Sammy snapped, as he white-knuckle-gripped his copy of the Prism the following week. He fell back and leaned against his locker to prop himself up at the shock of it all.

"That doesn't mean anything at all. He makes no sense, so don't worry about it for one second," Indigo said dismissively. "Benjamin isn't that bright — his elevator doesn't go all the way to the top floor if you know what I mean..." she chuckled.

Sammy let out a laugh. "That's great. Did you just make that up?"

"Yep!" Indigo fibbed, figuring Abuela wouldn't mind her borrowing her line.

"What's worse is he makes me sound like a total flower child! I don't even own any incense!" Indigo argued.

Sammy looked up from his paper with a side-eye glance in silent judgment.

"Okay, okay, my mom has some incense that I borrow from time to time. But I'm not a hippie!"

Sammy maintained his steadfast look at her.

"Okay, maybe I am! What's wrong with that?" She flipped her hair feathers to hide them behind her shoulders. "That's not the point! Who does he think he is to say this? He is so RUDE!"

"I know. This article isn't going to do any favors for him," Sammy said. "No one will support him after this! That's the best part about this article. Even though it is outrageous and mean, at least it will get him dropped by the BOTs. You can't talk to or about people like this and get away with it."

"No way. He's finished. I'm sure the BOTs will kick him out. They don't want a leader like that to represent them. Even if a few of Benjamin's cronies find this funny, Cleo and the other traditional kids won't support this — they are way too nice to go along with this cruelty." Indigo crumpled the paper in her backpack. "Do you think they will name Cleo as the new President? Could she do the job?"

"She *could* do it, but she doesn't have enough confidence to try. I'm guessing Cici would be the next leader. I hate to say it, but I'm not even sure that's an improvement over Benjamin!" Sammy said.

"Anything's an improvement over Benny," Indigo said emphatically. "And look at that stupid photo! Does he think there's one person who won't know it's a fake?"

Next to Megan's article entitled *Benjamin Rosa Gets EHS Back on Track,* Benjamin staged a photo where he was standing on the rock wall giving what looked like a very formal speech, with several heads in the foreground to make the venue look crowded. He was attempting to make it look like a candid snap captured at the Congregation.

However, fashion lovers Sammy and Indigo clearly knew it was a fake, as he was wearing different clothes than he had been wearing on that day.

Sammy shook his head, laughing. "I know, it's so stupid. Who even does that?" he said. He knew he could've pointed out the hypocrisy — after all he'd staged his own dramatic locker wreck for a Prism photo op just a few weeks ago — but, honestly, why ruin the moment?

"By the way, pull that paper back out, girl. Turn to page two."
Sammy opened his paper and pointed to a thin, photo-less article
running vertically down the gutter.

Indigo leaned in and saw that it was another article written by
Darla entitled *GLO Club Lights Up the BOT Darkness*. The article
highlighted how exciting it was that glow sticks that were handed
out at the end of the Congregation meeting, and Darla interviewed
different students about how they liked the sticks, and asked others
what they planned to do with theirs.

"That's nice, but why are glow sticks all she discusses? Why didn't
she mention what we stand for?" Indigo frustratedly questioned.

Sammy rolled his eyes, feeling unappreciated by Indigo yet again.
"Any press is good press. We knew the glow sticks would be a hit,
and it's great that they wrote an article about it. It is meaningful
too! We are light, they are dark." He smiled. "Oh! Also, they also
complimented your outfit in there, so that's amazing too!"

Indigo huffed disgustedly. "My outfit? Did they talk about
Benjamin's outfit in his article? Why do they always have to talk
about girls' looks?"

"Are you *ever* happy?" Sammy said, frustrated again at Indigo's
seeming lack of graciousness.

"No, no, you're right. Thanks for getting Darla to write that,"
she said, defeatedly.

Sammy went on. "What I want to know is why Benjamin is on
the front cover instead of us? And it isn't even an article about the
BOTs, it is just about him! Who cares about Benjamin anyway?"

He motioned for Indigo to follow him, leading her to the vicinity
of the principal's office.

"What are we doing?" she asked suspiciously. She slowed her pace
with each step closer to the principal's office, a place no student
wants to voluntarily go.

"I just want to grab a few more copies of the Prism to show off our article to the GLOs later." Sammy rushed through the crowd over to the newspaper stand and was aghast at what he saw.

All the newspapers were gone.

"How is this possible? There are always lots of papers left over at the end of the week. But now…on day one they are all taken? No way Benjamin's article was that popular!" Sammy was baffled.

"Who really cares, you can just show the GLO kids our copy…" Indigo was cut off by Sammy.

"No, no, no, but really, what is going on here?" He paused in pensive silence. "Oh, I know! I bet that bozo Benjamin had the BOT kids grab them all up. Maybe it is part of their uniform requirement to carry these around!"

He was relieved at the idea that BOT students were forced to take these. This was much more palatable than the horrifying alternative — that Benjamin was *this* massively popular.

Just then, Benjamin walked by Indigo and Sammy with his usual red swarm of BOTs walking behind him. "Hey guys," he said affably as he passed.

"HEY! Get back here!" Sammy yelled, beckoning Benjamin as he walked by. "What is this all about?" He held up the paper accusatorially.

"What is that?" Benjamin said, now several meters away.

"You know exactly what it is!" Sammy said.

Benjamin squinted his eyes and walked slowly back. "Oh, that's the Prism! Is my article in it today?" He excitedly snatched the paper from Sammy's hands.

Sammy was stunned. Could he really not know that his article was in here? Had he not seen the news yet? Is it possible that a paper with his face on it, and a nasty article about Sammy and Indigo, was so popular that every copy was gone within hours, without a massive conspiracy on Benjamin's part?

"Awesome!" Benjamin said. "We scored the cover!" he said, turning to Vinnie and Louie and giving them high fives. "Let's grab a bunch of copies for the BOT meeting later!" He went over to the empty newspaper stand and was instantly confused.

"Have they not put the papers out yet? How did you get this?" Benjamin asked.

Sammy had no idea how to respond. He couldn't bring himself to tell Benjamin that his article was the most popular thing to hit the Prism since news broke that Ms. Goldblum the Principal was dating Mr. Livermore, the gym teacher.

"I got it there this morning," he said, pointing to the newspaper stand.

"But…so…where are the rest?" Benjamin looked around the hallway and noticed that nearly every student who passed was holding one. His frown twisted into a self-righteous sort of shock-smile. "Wait, is it SOLD OUT?" He looked possibly even more stunned than Sammy had been at the achievement.

"We don't pay for the paper, so they aren't technically 'sold out.'" Sammy was grasping at straws to take away Benjamin's thunder, but it went in one ear and out the other.

"This is *epic*!" Benjamin started jumping up and down with his swarm of soccer teammates, chest bumping and high fiving and cheering in unison with the others.

Just then, Principal Goldblum, or Kitty to her friends, came out of her office to see what the commotion was about. "What's going on here?" she irately said.

"Sorry, Ms. Goldblum," Benjamin said softly. "Quick question for you. Are all the newspapers taken already?" He motioned down to the empty stand.

She looked as confused as the rest. "I guess so, yes. Wow, I've never seen that before!" She furrowed her brow. "I guess we could print more, but at this rate everyone who wants one should have one right?"

"I don't have one Ms. Goldblum, and I know a lot of my BOT Club members would want one too. If it isn't too much trouble, I'd love for you to print some more." Benjamin smiled charmingly.

"Okay, I'll have Kwame print out another batch. What was so popular in this issue anyway?" She took Sammy's copy from Benjamin and started looking it over.

"It's my article, ma'am," Benjamin said proudly.

She silently skimmed the article, and after a minute or so, she looked up at Benjamin with a disapproving look. "This certainly wasn't very nice of you Mr. Rosa. You don't want to get followers for your club by being nasty, do you? You can do better than this!"

"But Principal Goldblum, I just made a few harmless jokes. And as you said, it is the most popular issue of the Prism ever! Doesn't that say something? People want to see more of me!"

"Just because something is popular doesn't mean it is good," she said firmly. "Like drugs!" She looked proud of her quick-thinking simile.

"With respect, ma'am, I am not a drug, I'm just a super-handsome guy," Benjamin said with a wink, and a perplexingly flirtatious look in his eye.

At this point, if Sammy's piercing glare could shoot fire, Benjamin would be a toasted s'more.

He's flirting with a woman 30 years his senior? This guy has absolutely no radar for what's appropriate!

"Ms. Goldblum, I need to run, but could you please let me know when Kwame gets more printed? I *must* hand out more of these at the BOT meeting tomorrow." Benjamin took the folded paper from her hands and slapped it to Sammy's chest. "Thanks for hooking me up, bro," he said, taking Sammy's only copy of the paper with him.

For one of the first times in his life, Sammy was speechless. He couldn't bring himself to accept a reality where Benjamin's divisive and shock-and-awe rhetoric would be so widely accepted and popular. He knew that teens loved staring at a good social train wreck, but that couldn't possibly translate to something as important as school decorum or treatment of one another, could it?

The only explanation for the popularity of this issue had to be the tone — it was so over-the-top that everyone wanted to see it for themselves. The kids who liked his mean streak read it for laughs; the ones who didn't read it out of morbid curiosity. Was this really what got people's attention now? Bad news, no matter the cost?

Sammy looked back to the office to see that Ms. Goldblum had returned inside her office and was speaking to her assistant Kwame. She must be ordering more copies of Benjamin's hateful article. How could she support this?

Just then, Sammy realized he didn't even have his own copy anymore after Benjamin stole it, so he quickly changed his stance, now wanting those reprints. He noticed that in the kerfuffle, Indigo had left the scene too, probably to avoid a tussle with Benjamin.

As he started down the hallway to his next class, he heard a shout coming from down the hallway. "Hey, Rainbow Chaser!" A crowd cackled at the outburst from an unknown insulter.

Sammy continued walking, now with a purpose. He made a beeline directly to the classroom of Mr. Miller, the teacher who served as the advisor to the newspaper club.

This means war.

FIT TO PRINT

As Sammy entered the journalism classroom for the first time, which he now realized was more of a workshop than a classroom, he marveled at the eclectic batch of historical tools Mr. Miller used for his teaching. Directly to the right of the classroom entry door was a closed door labeled "Photography Dark Room." Sammy had always seen these on television, with their creepy red lighting and rows of dim black and white photographs that hung on a wire, fastened by clothespins and suspended above the room. He had no idea if that is how these rooms actually functioned, but the mystery behind that door mesmerized Sammy.

He was compelled to walk in and explore, but because of the large sign that read KEEP DOOR CLOSED, as well as his fear of Mr. Miller (his overreactions involving students' photography room missteps were a thing of legend), Sammy decided to control himself.

In the far corner, Sammy saw a large wooden table with many different compartments, each filled with silver antique letterpress letter blocks. Next to it, stood a large printing press stamp cabinet with many thin drawers stacked on top of one another.

But the clear centerpiece of the room was the vintage printing press that loomed large against the windows. Mr. Miller was tending to it, reaching deep into the machine for a reason unknown to Sammy. He could have been cleaning it or repairing it, Sammy wasn't sure.

The other corner of the room hosted a row of computers, printers, and scanners. It was a dizzying mix of old and new. The whole room looked like a journalistic version of Santa's workshop, and Sammy was enamored.

"Excuse me, Mr. Miller, could I please talk to you?" Intimidated in the presence of all these new and exciting master tools, inexplicably, Sammy felt the need to speak meekly.

Mr. Miller bumped his head as he pulled it from within the printing press. He had grease on his hands, and his white hair was now mussed from the impact. He wore a button up shirt with the sleeves rolled up, and dark pants that almost resembled jeans. A dark navy suit coat lay slung over his desk.

"Yeah, yeah, who's asking?" he said gruffly, not cranky in any way, just curtly direct as men of older generations often are. He walked over and shook Sammy's hand. Ink from his hand smeared onto Sammy's fingers and left a stain on his silver Moonstone ring. He looked down in horror. Mr. Miller noticed this dramatic display.

"Sorry about that, bud. Here," he handed Sammy his old, used, ink-covered rag that he pulled out of his back pocket. Sammy begrudgingly took it and began trying to wipe the ink from the formerly sparkling ring that adorned his manicured hand. It was a true debate whether this rag put more ink on his hands than it removed. He gave up and handed the rag back, and Mr. Miller returned it to his back pants pocket.

"I'm Sammy Iris. I'm the Director of the GLO Club." He felt pride at this distinction, which he assumed would be followed by accolades of admiration from Mr. Miller. Sammy figured that Mr. Miller had been closely following his social ascension as chronicled in the Prism and would now feel as if he was in the presence of royalty.

Mr. Miller's face furrowed. "The Director of *what*?"

Sammy's prideful, puffed-up chest deflated like a popped balloon.

"I need to talk to you about Benjamin Rosa," Sammy said.

"Who?" Mr. Miller said, again exhibiting his aloofness.

"Your reporter Megan Yamauchi wrote an article about him in this week's Prism…he's actually on the cover," Sammy said with an unintentional eye roll.

"Oh yeah, that tall redheaded kid. He started that robot club, right?" he said, wiping the ink off his hands with the old rag.

"BOT club, it stands for Back on Track…I'm not sure why he thinks the school is off track since you teachers are doing such a great job!" Sammy smiled a Cheshire grin, figuring a little flattery would do him no harm.

Mr. Miller stared at him blankly.

"…anyway, he wrote some terrible things in that article about me and Indigo Ortiz. He called me a rainbow chaser, and Indigo an incense-loving hippie. It was mean, and I don't think that he should be able to say things like that, especially in a school paper! You know?" Sammy stood tall, full of self-righteousness.

Who could possibly disagree with that?

Mr. Miller walked over and sat down on top of a student's desk, throwing his one leg over it and propping himself up with the other. "Yes and no, Sammy, yes and no."

Was he kidding? Could there actually be a debate in his mind if Benjamin's slander was acceptable?

Sammy couldn't hold back his disdain. "I don't understand…he is rude and nasty, and there are even flat-out lies in there!"

"Well now, *that's* a problem. What did he lie about?" Mr. Miller looked concerned.

"For starters, that photo is fake! That wasn't taken at the Congregation. He set that up later. And then, he says that his online 'say no to drugs' thing resulted in 100% of the student body being drug-free. Like…what does that even mean? How could he claim that?"

"Hmm…" Mr. Miller rubbed his leathery tan chin in thought. "This is a tough one. What do you suggest we do?"

Sammy didn't skip a beat. "I suggest he be permanently banned from being covered by the paper, of course! In fact, I'd like to see the BOT club completely shut down. They are dangerous, all of them!"

"*All* of them?" He paused to allow Sammy to take back his superlative. Mr. Miller realized after several seconds of deafening silence that a retraction was most certainly not forthcoming.

"Now listen, Stevie, I have several of these kids in my class. I know because they are always wearing red. It tricks me into thinking I'm angry, because I'm seeing red all the time!" He chuckled to himself at his corny joke.

Sammy was not amused. "Sammy."

"What?"

"My name is Sammy, not Stevie." Sammy crossed his arms and felt his mouth starting to purse up, the first of his unintentional body language signs that he was mentally shutting down.

"What I'm asking is, do you really think that *all* the BOT club members are dangerous? What about that little friend of yours, Christy?"

"You mean Cleo? I barely know her," Sammy snipped grumpily.

Mr. Miller made a face of bafflement. "I think you're forgetting that I oversee the yearbook too. You two used to be on every other page together, as thick as thieves for years! What happened?" he said, looking concerned.

"Nothing!" Sammy said defensively. He sat there, feeling Mr. Miller's gaze burning onto his head as he avoided eye contact and looked at the ground. Sammy could feel boiling anger build up in his chest, crawl up to warm his neck, flush onto his cheeks, and run down his arms and into his hands, bathing them in a cold, clammy sweat.

After a while, he was forced to break the silence. He erupted.

"Fine! This! *This* is what happened!" he said, motioning around the room. "Your *paper* is what happened! The *BOTs* are what happened! Our *clubs* are what happened! *Benjamin* is what happened! I hate it!"

Sammy felt tears of anger welling up in his eyes as he panted from the emotionally exhausting rant.

Mr. Miller changed the subject quickly, attempting to bring down Sammy's skyrocketing blood pressure. "Come here. Do you see this?" He walked him over to a framed poster on the wall. The poster read:

FIVE PRINCIPLES
OF ETHICAL JOURNALISM
1. Accuracy and Truth
2. Minimize Harm
3. Act Independently
4. Transparency and Accountability
5. Fairness and Impartiality

Sammy walked over and perused the poster, not sure what all of this meant. He noticed that below each principle, there was a small description of each category. If he had more time, or care, reading this likely would have helped to clear up his confusion. But he didn't, on either account.

"Yeah, so?"

He realized this may not have been the most respectful tone to use with a teacher. "I mean, yes, Mr. Miller I see this. What about it?"

Marginally better.

"These are our sacred principles of ethical journalism. Everything we do here, with the Prism as well as the yearbooks and other publications, must adhere as closely as possible to these principles. These are not just things that our publications must uphold, but our *journalists* must uphold as well."

He walked over and pointed at a 'Staff Wall' that displayed each of his student reporters' names and photos.

"Every reporter, including Darla and Megan who have been my main point people for the club reporting, as well as the rest of the newspaper team — Luanna, Eliza, Cole, Leo, Nolan, Arlo, Lidia, and Ruthie Marie — every single one must take and maintain a journalistic oath to these principles. These ethics guide everything we do here, Mr. Iris. I take them *very* seriously. If we as journalists were to abandon them, well, I shudder to consider how our school could function." Mr. Miller gazed off in the distance with a worried look in his eye.

Sammy knew all these kids, and from what he could tell, this is a group of honest and fair people. But that didn't mean he could trust them. Any of them.

"I'm not saying you are doing anything wrong, Mr. Miller. But there is no way that some of your reporters are living up to those rules. That article was *not* true, *not* fair, *did not* minimize harm. Since Megan wrote that article, I have kids yelling 'rainbow chaser' at me everywhere I go!" he said, defeatedly.

"I'm sorry to hear that, Sammy. That is regrettable and I'm sorry. Let's explore this a little more. So, you feel that several of the principles of journalism were breached with this article, yes? Do you think that Benjamin, the subject of the article who gave the information, or my reporter Megan, is responsible?"

"BOTH!" Sammy instantly shouted. He paused to consider the question after his knee-jerk reaction. "I don't know…yes, I'd say both, because it is Benjamin's responsibility to tell the truth, and Megan's responsibility to find out if what she's reporting is true."

"As the head of the paper, is it my fault too?" Mr. Miller questioned.

"I already said it wasn't, *geez*," Sammy said sheepishly.

"You can tell the truth."

Sammy paused, trying to figure out if this was a trick or not. "Well, maybe a little. I mean, we should be able to trust the paper to report the truth." Sammy's tone softened a bit. He had never had a conversation quite like this before, where an adult actually talked to him like a peer. He was engaged, suspicious, and confused all at the same time.

"You should, indeed, be able to trust us." Mr. Miller smiled for the first time in this interaction. It was clear that he was relishing this teachable moment, which Sammy considered "yet to be taught," as it wasn't clear where this was going.

"In this case, Sammy, I would say that in the real world, the primary responsibility of accuracy would lie with the reporter. Most publications aren't as sophisticated as something like *The New Yorker* where they have a team of fact-checkers. For the leaders of small newspapers, we need to be able to trust our reporters to ensure the accuracy of their articles. Ultimately it is my responsibility as the news leader if something they put out is wrong, but it is simply impossible for me to read everything and do a deep dig fact check into every detail of every article. The most important thing for me to do is hold them accountable if I find out something isn't right."

"Then it is Megan's fault! I am going to give her a piece of my mind at recess tomorrow!" Sammy was filled with anticipation at taking his frustration out on someone.

"Not so fast, Mr. Iris." Mr. Miller stood up, clasped his hands behind his back, and began pacing in that teacher-like-way, as if he was lecturing a class.

"First of all, we are not a professional newspaper. All my reporters are learning their craft from me, and any mistakes they make are attributable to me. This is a classroom, and in this room, I am responsible."

Sammy realized it would be tougher to rub a teacher's face in his mess, but he was willing to try.

"Secondly, and more importantly, let's talk for a moment about *your* article last week in the Prism."

Sammy gulped.

"I read Darla's scathing article about Benjamin and his club, and your personal victimization at the hands of the BOTs. Am I summarizing that correctly?"

Sammy smirked. So, Mr. Miller *had* been bluffing when he said he didn't know who he was. Trying to stay neutral, maybe? Either way, Sammy felt vindicated. His fame clearly reached farther than Mr. Miller was willing to admit.

"Yes, I was a victim at the hands of him. The difference there, though, is that everything in my article was 100% true! As I said, he's dangerous!"

"Interesting," Mr. Miller said. "Because last week I had a very similar conversation to the one we are having now with a BOT student who felt your article was a near-total fabrication. Now granted, yours had less outright insults or direct statistical claims that are more than likely false, however, yours was full of innuendo and insinuations that bordered on what we call 'slander' in my business. Not to mention, I heard your photo was fabricated or exaggerated, much like Benjamin's. Is this true?"

"Uh…I…no…but…" Sammy stammered over his words as he struggled to find the best way to say *I'm nothing like Benjamin!* while also being honest, which would require him to admit that he is, in fact, somewhat similar to Benjamin.

The thought left a poisonously bitter taste in his mouth. Then his mind circled back to an earlier tidbit. Who was the BOT student who reported him to Mr. Miller? Who hated him enough to do such a thing?

"Look, Sammy, I don't mean to put you on the spot. You don't need to answer me now, but…" Sammy cut him off.

"Who reported me?"

"Now you know I can't divulge that information, in the same way that I will keep your identity protected too regarding this conversation. That is the number one rule of journalism: protect your sources." He smirked. "I just mentioned that because they went as far as asking me to report you to Principal Goldblum for a violation of student conduct. I didn't do that of course, but I wanted you to understand that while you are hurt and frustrated by Benjamin's article, quite similarly your actions had a harmful impact on other students that you were clearly unaware of."

"Reporting me to Ms. Goldblum? That's crazy! If you could just tell me who…"

"Sammy, the point I'm trying to make is a classic one. Teddy Roosevelt once said, 'Avoid the base hypocrisy of condemning in one man, what you pass over in silence when committed by another.'"

Sammy stared at him blankly. Mr. Miller chuckled.

"In simpler terms, you can't criticize someone for an action that you would allow, or stay silent about, when you or someone on your side does the same thing. It's basically a fancy version of 'people who live in glass houses shouldn't throw stones.' Have you heard that one?"

"Yeah, basically I shouldn't judge someone if I am doing something similar," Sammy pouted.

"Exactly. Society is addicted to being the victim. Everyone is fluent in the art of how others have done them wrong. Rarely do they look at what they themselves have done wrong, often from what turns out to be nearly identical offenses. If they do notice the irony, it is usually written off as 'he started it' finger-pointing, yet timelines can never support both sides firing the first cannon."

Mr. Miller walked over to the desk where Sammy was sitting slumped and defeated like a ragdoll. With his dampened emotion came a loss of energy as well.

There will be no need for gymnastics in the empty gym today!

Mr. Miller looked at his watch. "You missed your whole recess for this! I hope this helped you, and that it all makes sense."

Sammy sat cross-armed in silence.

"The point is, with journalism, you are right that it is imperative for us to uphold the journalistic ethic. Sadly, we should expect that the subjects of our stories are probably stretching or twisting the truth in some way or another for their benefit. It happens when widespread exposure is involved, that the interviewee always wants to look good. Like you and Benjamin. I get it. Vanity and power corrupt all things."

Mr. Miller was putting Sammy and Benjamin in the same category? Sammy felt a ball of vomit crawl up and land in his throat, sitting there, mocking him.

Mr. Miller got up and walked to the door with Sammy at his side. "It is up to *all* of us to ensure that truth is at the center of all that we do."

He began counting off on his fingers as he made each point. "It is up to the *individuals* to demand unbiased truth from the news, not just the parts they want to hear. It is up to the *reporters* to take pride in what they put their names on, and to remove any personal bias from their reporting to share facts, not opinions dressed up as facts. And it is up to the *news* as a whole to truly understand the importance of their power in shaping minds, communities, and the overarching world. After all, if we lose commitment to truth and integrity, what else is left?"

He patted Sammy on the shoulder and walked back into his room as the bell rang. Like a wise old turtle, Mr. Miller disappeared back into the shell of darkness under his printing press, while Sammy disappeared into the buzzing hive of the hallways, still trying to wipe ink off his Moonstone ring.

SPECIAL DELIVERY

Saturdays can be boring when you are an only child. Thankfully, Sammy's mom and dad were always happy to include him in their respective chores...and how *enthralling* the choices were!

Today, Option One offered Sammy the chance to help his mom clean out a spare bedroom which used to be beautifully organized, but after years of neglect, now had boxes and clothes piled up the walls like crawling ivy.

She could be like a dog with a bone on a project like this. It took a while for her to find the time and motivation to tackle a project like this, but once it started, it was never done until it was *done*. This sounded exhausting for Sammy.

Alternatively, Option Two would send him outside to help his father on one of his yardwork adventures...actually, more like debacles.

Alex Iris had always been a city guy — "a real city slicker," as the locals liked to tease. He'd spent his whole life surrounded by concrete and coffee shops before deciding that a few acres of open land might be good for the soul.

The soul, maybe. His pride? Not so much.

Nearly every week there was another "incident." Whether he sunk his mower into a muddy hole in the yard and had to get the neighbor to tow him out, ran over a fence with his huge snowblower, or injured himself trying to trap pesky animals that were hunting his beloved chickens, doing yard chores with Alex was never dull.

And because of the inevitable chaos that always happened, Sammy could often disappear to do something more fun without being seen.

Sammy pondered his options this bright, sunny Saturday. He decided that he'd go and help his dad. At least he could get some fresh air, and he figured he could probably sneak away to take a dip in Miss Stella's pool without him noticing. It was very convenient to have a neighbor with a pool that big who travels that much.

He put on his barn shoes, pulled out his waistband, and glanced into the darkness of his shorts to ensure he had on boxers in case he needed an impromptu swimsuit. He stepped out of the door, grabbed his scooter, and began rolling and dashing around the walkways near the house and into the barn.

Because his driveway was an old windy gravel path, he couldn't successfully ride his scooter, skateboard, or hoverboard down it without being catapulted from any device by the jagged pieces of stone. As a work-around, he had gotten good at navigating the few paved sidewalks and walkways near the house, practicing his stunts, flips and twists on the device of the day. The real fun was going wild as he flew across the smooth cement floors inside the barn.

"What's up, Sammy!" Alex said, hunkered over the lawn mower, looking perplexed at why it wouldn't turn on.

"How's it going there, dad?"

"I'm a little frustrated. I'm not sure why this isn't working. I've taken this whole thing apart and reconstructed it, but it still doesn't work. I've been watching videos online but can't seem to see what is going on. I'll get it, though!" he said optimistically, hoping to convince himself as well as Sammy. "Hey, can you do me a favor?"

Sammy gave a long, drawn-out sigh. "Fiiinee, what?"

"Can you run to the end of the driveway and drag the garbage can back to the house? I need to mow there later and want that out of the way."

Sammy dramatically started stomping out of the barn. "Oh, and grab the mail too, please!" Alex shouted after him.

When you live on an old farming estate that is set hundreds of feet away from the street, the experience of garbage pick-up and drop-off is a giant production. The house was built in the 1800s, and back then it's safe to say that the builders hadn't considered the future difficulties encountered by modern people when schlepping huge, wheeled garbage cans back and forth down a gravel driveway. Then again, they probably would have relished in the convenience of having a magical woman or man come and pick up your trash right from your house, making it disappear into thin air.

Perspective was an amazing thing.

Sammy stomped and huffed his way down the driveway, performing for an audience that didn't exist. Still, the show must go on. With a driveway this long, the trip felt endless — especially when you were a gangly teenager dragging a large green garbage can up a bumpy gravel path. He'd shot up a few inches this year and finally stood taller than the can, but that didn't make it any easier to handle. The thing was awkward and heavy, and finding the perfect angle to keep it from tipping — or rolling straight into the lake that ran alongside the driveway — was a full-blown science experiment.

He reached the end of the driveway, snatched the can roughly, and started back. About halfway through his bumping and fumbling journey back to the house, he realized he had forgotten something.

The mail.

He abandoned the can and walked again back to the end of the driveway to collect it, all the while inspecting the damage done to his manicure.

He flipped open the mailbox door and noticed that the box was full, which aggravated him even more, as the prospect of having to balance both the mail *and* the garbage can seemed simply too inhumane to bear.

He decided to go through the mail and see if he could throw anything away, so he'd have less to carry. He started leafing through the mail, not exactly sure what his parents considered valuable or junk mail, and frankly, not caring all that much.

Suddenly, a shiny, metallic gold envelope caught his eye. *Fancy!* he marveled. He flipped it forwards and backwards, admiring how its subtle sparkle shimmered in the light. The envelope was bulkier than the average piece of mail, which peaked Sammy's interest even more. As he turned to examine the front side again, he looked at the return address.

Reginald Arco.

Sammy had no idea what Cleo's dad would be sending to his family. Maybe an apology letter for what a brat his kid has been.

Sammy tried to put on his tough-guy armor, but deep down he was only filled with nerves and sentimentality at the thought of a reconnection with Cleo. But, he figured he had to stay strong.

Better to be safe than sappy.

Sammy's curiosity was overflowing now. It was all he could do to restrain from opening the envelope, but he knew his mom well enough to know that you don't open her mail.

He looked down the envelope and saw that it was addressed to "Mr. and Mrs. Alex Iris." He giggled to himself. He knew how peeved his mom Mac would be at seeing this old-fashioned verbiage — that reduced her to simply a "Mrs." without a name — as she *always* was when formal letters came in like this. Sammy marveled at how she never ceased to be surprised and angered each time it happened, and how every single time, it elicited an emotional reaction as fresh as the first.

He abandoned the garbage can halfway down the driveway and ran inside to the house. He clomped upstairs, still in his outdoor shoes, and knocked on the door of the spare room his mother was attempting to reorganize.

"Mom?"

"Lleno, I'm busy, can you come back…"

"I *need* to talk to you!" Sammy implored.

"Fine, come in…carefully!"

Sammy turned the knob and pushed on the door, meeting resistance immediately. Once he pried the door open a crack, he could see that there were clothes and shoes and boxes piled throughout the room. The vertical ivy-like vines of clutter had disappeared, and now everything was on ground level. He could only barely get the door open wide enough to slip into the room.

Mac looked down at his feet. "Sammy, what have I told you about wearing your muddy shoes in the house? Take them off!"

"Fine, *whatever!*" He rolled his eyes and kicked them out of the room, aggravated that she didn't grasp the importance of the news he had to share.

He handed her the gold envelope.

She looked down at it and immediately looked perplexed. "I'm not sure why you are giving this to me. This is for dad, and someone named Mrs. Dad. I didn't know there was a female named 'Alex Iris' in town, but maybe that's possible. Alex *can* be a woman's name too. What I know for sure is that this isn't for me! Nope, my name is nowhere here — just Mr. and Mrs. Alex Iris!"

She flipped the envelope back to Sammy with annoyance as she huffed and rolled her eyes. It hit the ground next to his feet, shimmering in the sunshine.

Sammy chuckled as he watched her face getting redder as she stood there.

"I mean it is *inconceivable* that in modern times you still speak about women as property of a man! Can you imagine someone calling you Mr. or Mrs. Someone Else? It is beyond my comprehension." She let out a frustrated growl.

"Are you done?" Sammy said, laughing and patting her on the shoulder.

"Get off of me, you little instigator," she said, smirking but still fuming.

"While I've been enjoying the latest episode of *The Mom Freakout Show*, I actually wanted you to look at the mail. Look who it's from."

"Reginald, hmm, I wonder what this could be." She ripped the envelope open gently, careful to preserve it. She pulled out one of the cards from inside, and as she did silver and gold confetti fluttered from the envelope down to the ground, adding sparkle to the cluttered floor and its contents. She smiled as she read the card.

"Well, what is it?" Sammy barked in anticipation.

"They're getting married!" she said happily.

Sammy was speechless from confusion. He knew Cleo wasn't marrying her father...was she? Nothing else made any sense.

Not that Cleo marrying her dad would make sense either.

"She's sweet, they'll be really happy together. I'm so happy for him!" Mac smiled and ruffled the hair on Sammy's head as she read cards and inserts that continued to pour out of the clown car envelope.

"Mom, what are you talking about? Who is 'nice?'"

"Hold on, I just want to call your dad quickly." She put the phone to her ear. "I'm sure he won't hear his phone if he's in the barn... oh, hey honey!" She put up her index finger to Sammy, asking for a minute before they resumed their conversation. "Guess what?" She paused dramatically, smiling. The smile faded. "No, I don't know anything about an ignition coil. Do you think I snuck out there at night and played around under your mower for giggles? Forget about that for a minute because…fine, I'll send him out in a second to help. But first I have some exciting news! Reginald is getting married!" Her face was beaming with delight. "Yes, they will be great together. It has been so long for him."

Who is good for him? Who is he marrying? How was Sammy the only one that didn't know about this?

"Okay love you, yes, I'll send him out in a second. Bye." Mac hung up the phone and turned to Sammy. "Sorry honey, what were you saying?"

"Who is Reginald marrying?"

She looked at him with an inquisitive look. "You can't be…I mean, are you serious?" She cocked her head sideways and a face of deep concern washed over her face.

It was becoming clear to Mac in this moment that Sammy had grossly misrepresented the situation with Cleo to her, and that in reality she was very unaware about how distanced the kids had become. She was frustrated at him for deceiving her, and yet extremely sympathetic at the level of estrangement that had developed between him and his best friend. She touched his shoulder.

"Honey, Reginald has been dating a woman named Genevieve, Viv as she likes to be called, for months now. He told me that Cleo has been having a really hard time with it. She has been hanging out with those kids at the church a lot more to avoid the house, I guess Viv's there quite a bit. I wonder how she's taking the engagement news…"

Sammy didn't know what to say. His mind toggled at the speed of light between confusion, denial, anger at Cleo for not telling him about any of this, and he even felt compassion for his friend.

This was the nail in the coffin. The final eye-opener he needed. This truly was the first time that Sammy realized how far the two of them had let this silly feud go. He was missing out on Cleo's life. She was missing out on his. They hadn't been there for one another for so much of this year, and all because of their allegiances to clubs that certainly didn't care about them. How could they have let this happen?

At that moment, Sammy vowed to end this ridiculous fight with Cleo. He missed his best friend. He knew she missed him too. He often caught her stealing glances at him in the lunchroom or the hallway, attempting to be covert as she tried to hide her laughter at one antic or another that he was performing. When he noticed her doing this, he had always chosen to snap his glance back without a smile or acknowledgment that she was there. This was the most successful move he could think of to keep her wanting more, yet at an arm's length.

Letting her get any closer was excruciating for him.

But things were about to change. Sammy was going to that wedding. Wild dogs couldn't keep him away. He knew he had to be the one to extend the olive branch, or their relationship may never recover. He was a little resentful that she had not tried to patch things up throughout this whole situation — other than her "let's put the past in the past thing" — whatever that was.

He had never once been the first to attempt an apology to someone else, but there's a first time for everything.

"Did I get invited?" Sammy said sheepishly. His whole plan depended on it.

Mac looked down at the RSVP card. "Of course you did, honey! Do you want to go? Your father and I want to be there to support Reginald. You're welcome to come, but I understand if you don't want to. We can have Grandma Nancy come over and hang out with you. Your choice, Pep!"

He paused, knowing this was his last chance to back away from what would otherwise be a very mature, and challenging move of contrition.

"When is it?" Sammy asked.

She glanced at the pile of cards. "It is in less than a month! Wow that is quick. Probably the advantage of leading your own church — you can mobilize things much quicker than the Average Joe. What do you say?" she said smiling at Sammy.

"If I don't have any better plans, I suppose I'll go," he managed to eke out. "I'll check my calendar and get back to you, but for now, put me down as a yes. I can always cancel later."

"Your *calendar*?" Mac chuckled, seeing right through this playing-hard-to-get charade.

"Mom, stoooppp," Sammy said, running briskly out of the room and across the hall into his bedroom, hoping she'd forget he was there so he could get out of chore duty altogether.

As he laid on his bed under the covers, he glanced over to what he calls his "Fashion Corner," where he has a mirror set up with big bulbs around it like in the movies, and a white fur-lined chair pushed against the mirror's attached vanity. The vanity had creams, art supplies, fabric samples, and sports equipment spread across it. On the chair and floor were an assortment of team jerseys, shirts, pants, scarves and every other type of clothing that you could imagine.

Then, his eyes fixated on a shimmering silver speck of glitter that caught the light, peeking out from under the pile of clothes on the vanity. He knew just what it was.

He walked slowly over to the vanity, pushed the clothing to the side, and picked up the item. It was a sequin covered picture frame that he had made at Cleo's birthday party last year from the zoo party. They were laughing hysterically and wearing intricate face paint, looking like they just stepped out of a Broadway performance of Cats — Sammy was painted as a white tiger, and Cleo was a cheetah. They both had headbands on with matching cat ears to complement their looks.

Sammy stared at the photo, bringing it close to his face, examining the image of the shared joy between him and his former best friend. He clutched the photo to his chest and tears began to well up in his eyes.

He paused to blame Benjamin in his mind, accusing him of ruining his whole life with the initiation of these clubs. But right now, he was overwhelmed with such sadness, that even insulting Benjamin couldn't make him feel happy right now. And the truth was, he wasn't even sure that Benjamin deserved all the ire Sammy had been sending his way.

But to consider that thought was too much enlightenment for one day.

The reflection of his own face in the glass of the frame made him pause momentarily, reflecting on his friendship and love of Cleo.

He missed her face. He missed her dorky jokes. He missed gossiping and trading jabs with her.

He was suddenly shocked out of his daydream.

"Remember your dad needs you in the barn!" his mom shouted across the hall.

Of course, he does. It doesn't get better than lawnmower repair on a Saturday!

This day just keeps getting better.

SUNDAY SPA DAY

"Sun-day, Spa-day!" Sammy's mom chanted as she marched around the house rhythmically clapping. This used to be a chant that Sammy and Mac would do together, but being at the high school now, he felt he was much too cool be a part of something like that.

To be clear, he was much too cool for the *chanting*. He would never be too cool for pampering.

He was only flesh and blood.

Spa day didn't usually even mean going to the spa, it was shorthand for mother/son time. Because they both enjoyed a good indulgence, some Sundays it *could* refer to a literal spa day, complete with a manicure or pedicure visit at the local day spa. But most days it just meant a trip to the lake to sit on the beach and watch the birds or mock the inappropriately skimpy outfits of the swimmers and fellow beachgoers, depending on the season.

It could also mean simple things like a trip to the store for shopping, lunch, and browsing the bookstore. The point was for them to spend some gab-and-relax time together, and it was secretly the favorite day of the week for them both. While Sammy called Cleo his best friend, the fact was that his mom Mac was truly his closest confidant, and the one he most hoped to emulate in his life.

Mac came from this town, however she grew up in the perfectly manicured middle-class village part of town, so farm life was as new to her as anyone else. After high school, Mac had moved to the big city for her undergrad and master's degrees, where she also met Alex and the two had lived for more than a decade. They decided to relocate the family from the city back to her small hometown when Sammy was five years old to give him a simpler life. It seemed growingly difficult to provide an "unplugged" upbringing for a child, but his parents were committed to trying.

"Pick your poison! What would you like to do today?" Mac looked at Sammy, eager to inspire a little pep in his step. He had been pouting around the house for what seemed like forever, and only yesterday did she fully understand why — the deep division between he and Cleo had been so much worse than she thought. Mac couldn't let this go unspoken another day without checking in on him.

"I don't care," he said, grumpily pulling on his rainbow shoes. "Do we have to go? I'm tired," he huffed.

Mac looked at him with her mouth agape. "*My* Sammy is trying to get out of Spa Day? What's next, you stop styling your hair?"

Sammy audibly gasped. "What kind of animal do you think I am?!" he laughed.

Mac grabbed his hands and examined them. "From the looks of it, you need a manicure touch-up. It looks like a wolverine was gnawing on your hands! Did you wrestle the McMinn's Great Dane, Atari, and I didn't know it?"

"Don't you know that it is an unwritten rule to *never* make fun of a guy's manicure? Didn't dad teach you anything about men?"

Alex piped up from the other room. "Yeah, have some class! Hey, maybe I'll come too! Can they do some Cleveland sports team colors on me?"

Sammy turned to his mom with a mocking face. "Yeah, I'd say the Browns football colors would be just gorgeous. Orange and brown. Perrrrfect," he said rolling his eyes. "Perfectly *hideous*!"

"How *dare* you insult my Browns!" Alex put on his best fake offense. "Okay I'm in, let's go!" Alex started to get up, mockingly turning off the TV and getting ready.

"What a dope!" Sammy laughed and gave his dad a hug. "Bye, Dad."

"Byeeee!" Alex said in a sing-songy voice, waving his fingers fancily at them.

Then, for no reason at all, Alex began running after them, growling like a lion pursuing its prey. As Mac and Sammy ran screaming from him, heading towards the front door, they suddenly heard a loud thump, and looked back to see that he tripped over a pair of his own sloppily discarded shoes and fell to the ground. He frequently did pratfalls and jokes like this, so Mac and Sammy couldn't tell for sure if this one was real or fake. Either way, they didn't have time to find out. There were fingernails to paint!

They dashed out the door and hopped in the car. As they started down their long driveway, Sammy exclaimed, "Oh no, here he goes again!"

"What?" Mac looked around confused.

Sammy nudged Mac and pointed to the rear-view mirror. They both looked to see Alex lumbering down the driveway behind the car, continuing the groaning and moaning performance of Frankenstein-on-a-bender. Even though Sammy felt he was much too old for nonsense like this from when he was a kid, he still couldn't help but smile.

"Now you know why I need some time away!" Mac exclaimed, laughing at Alex's antics and beeping the horn as they drove away.

For rural folks, country roads were like old, reliable friends. You knew they are always there; you saw them often, you rarely took special note that they existed, but you also knew that you couldn't live life without the comfort of them. Mac and Sammy rumbled down one of the hundreds of these familiar old roads that twist like veins wrapped around the countryside. Along the way, they passed the landmarks of their daily commute — the college, the golf course, one of Emerald's hotels, and a countless number of nameless estates, farms, and old abandoned factories.

Suddenly, traffic came to a near crawl. That could only mean one thing. Sammy stuck his head out of the window, and about four cars ahead of them he could see the telltale black square cart of an Amish buggy led by a bouncing horse head, with the cart's big black wheels turning as fast as the horse could pull it.

"Pass them!" Sammy barked, exhibiting a much-too-young case of road rage.

"Lleno, I can't barrel by four cars *and* a buggy without running into oncoming traffic. Just simmer down!" Mac gripped the wheel with white knuckles, trying to set a good example by tempering her own impatience.

Being that they were on a two-lane road, their only choice was to lurch along until each of the cars ahead of them had found an opening that would allow them to pass the cart. After what seemed like an eternity to a very impatient teen, they finally pulled up directly behind the buggy.

Mac was a rather aggressive driver — city driving had not worn off when they returned to small-town living — so the minute that the oncoming traffic had lapsed, she pulled the car into the oncoming lane, briskly passing the cart.

Whenever they passed an Amish buggy, Sammy loved gazing around the blinders on the horses' faces to stare directly at their huge, black round eyes and long eyelashes. He always wondered what the horse was thinking. Was she happy to be out and running? Did she feel trapped and oppressed at being a beast of burden? Was she only thinking about food and sleep (the same short list of concerns that plagued Sammy's dad too)?

This time, the same as every time, the horse kept her answers to herself.

They got around the cart and began to hum along again, nearing the center of town on their way to the day spa.

"Oh no, look at this. Ah, what a shame for Jimmy, losing the store." Mac squinted, trying to read a large handwritten sign in the old hardware store window as they drove by. Her face fell. "Wow, I can't believe he put that up."

Sammy twisted his neck to see the sign out the back of his window as they moved along with traffic.

Closed Permanently Thanks to the Incompetence of
Mayor Moron and His Band of Merry Yes Men

Sammy slapped his hand over his mouth, trying to hold back laughter at the brashness of such a move. He knew his mom wouldn't find it funny, knowing how desperate and angry her friend Jimmy must be to write such a scathing public message. Still, Sammy couldn't help himself from finding a little joy in Jimmy's attempt at sticking-it-to-the-man.

"Poor Jimmy," was all Sammy could utter.

Passing through Emerald's small-town downtown was a mix of emotions for Mac. Over her last four decades or so of life, she had watched the town go from a bustling thoroughfare to a ghost town during several market crashes, to rebounding back with entrepreneurial spirit.

Back and forth it goes.

This was one of the ebb years, where things were tough after various industries left the area, and the town was struggling.

Sammy looked up and realized that they were just about to pass by "The Graveyard." He felt the silent tension grow in the car. You could cut it with a chainsaw. He was surprised that Mac had taken this route, as she usually tried to go a different way to avoid the memories. Maybe today she was feeling good about it.

Nope.

Sammy glanced at his mom and saw tears beginning to well up in her eyes.

"The Graveyard" was Sammy's mental nickname for his parents' old business building. Their beautiful office had been here on Main Street here in Emerald, and while they still owned the building, it now sat empty since the company's closure during the pandemic, like a graveyard honoring the former workers, the mission of the company, and Mac and Alex's dream of 15 years.

While she put on a brave face, every time they passed it, Sammy saw Mac's eyes fill with tears, her hands gripping the steering wheel a little tighter. He would gently rub her back silently offering support, careful not to ask anything, to avoid causing her pain by forcing her to find words to speak about the deep wounds of the loss.

"Thanks, honey. I'm good," she said, tapping his hand on her shoulder, putting on a brave face as always.

The commercial buildings that lined Emerald's Main Street were squished together like sardines, one pushed into another. They had very ornate and historic facades, each one with unique woodworking, window designs, and other quirky features that indicated the various decades that they were built or updated.

Small town Main Streets are like EPCOT Center timelines of the country's various architectural styles, all rolled into single roads.

At the town's central stop light, Sammy's mom beeped the horn and waved. He noticed out the front window that his teacher, Ms. Traben, was crossing the road, waving feverishly in the front window at him. He raised a hand and offered her a subtle wave, not wanting to look too eager. He then turned his gaze and looked out the side window and saw his neighbor Miss Stella walking with her family into the coffee shop.

Guess he had those vacation days wrong. Thank goodness he didn't show up to her pool in his underwear yesterday!

Everywhere you looked, you saw a familiar face.

Welcome to Emerald.

"We're here!" Mac chirped as they pulled into the day spa parking lot. Sammy looked down at his hands, embarrassed at how tragic they looked. He instinctively curled his fingers up into fists to hide his shame.

As they entered the spa, the little gold bell attached to the door jingled. Inside the spa, there were friends and acquaintances from wall to wall. Sammy heard many greet him, greet his mother, ask how his last soccer game went, ask him about his dating status, the list went on. He walked along aloofly, acknowledging no one. He had strategically put his ear buds in his ears before entering to avoid being a part of the town's endless obligatory chattering, yet he was careful not to have any music on so he could still eavesdrop.

One downside of small-town life is that your secrets are *never* your own.

No one else's are their own either.

Sammy and Mac had regular seats at the nail salon area, and they walked right in and claimed them without needing an appointment. Sammy had picked a clear polish for his nails today, because he was feeling a little flat. Drained. Monochromatic.

Mac picked a color called "*Indigo* Blue."

Ironic.

As they sat there, getting manicures and pedicures, Mac tried to unravel what was going on with Sammy and Cleo. "So, how have things been at school?"

"Fine," Sammy said curtly.

"Lleno, come on. What's going on with Cleo? Have you guys made up yet?"

"There's nothing to make up for. She made her choice, so she can live with it. She's a BOT now. Believe me, that's punishment enough for her."

Sammy was very hesitant to talk about his feelings, mainly because he didn't trust that he wouldn't start to tear up. The last thing he needed was the nail shop gossip gang to start spreading the news all around town that he was crying over Cleo.

Mac continued to push, so in a whisper, he explained to her all about the development of the clubs but avoided mention of Indigo or Benjamin altogether. Sammy knew if he told her that this all started because Cleo aligned with his enemy Benjamin, then Mac would want to know why Sammy didn't like Benjamin. Then Sammy would have to explain how Benjamin bullied and mocked him for being fancy, and Mac would be infuriated that Sammy was being teased for being himself — a "beautiful butterfly in a world of moths" — as she called him. He knew that she would then probably go and tell Principal Goldblum or confront Benjamin's parents or something equally embarrassing, and all of that was just way too much for Sammy to handle in his fragile state.

"That's all you're getting from me! Now give me a break. *Please* mom."

"Okay, Sammy, I'll back off. But just know that friends like Cleo don't come along very often, and I would hate to see you lose someone so important in your life over something this silly." She reached over and carefully held his still drying painted hand.

"I know, mom. Thanks. It'll work itself out with us."

These are the only words he could muster up to offer her today. Sammy hoped that he had done a good job of convincing her.

The only thing he knew for sure was that he had definitely *not* convinced himself.

Just then, the door's bell jingled. Sammy glanced up at the door. Benjamin. And his father.

What on earth is he...

"Hello, we are here for our *sports massages*," Wyatt barked out loudly, ensuring that everyone heard the oh-so-manly reason they were there.

"Isn't that..." Wyatt lowered his voice as he leaned over to Benjamin, looking over at Sammy and Mac. Benjamin looked over and gave an incognito friendly wave to Sammy, then seemingly joined his father in mocking the scene.

"Oh look, Sammy! There's your friend Benjamin." Mac motioned to Wyatt and Benjamin to come over. They headed over, looking as happy as Sammy was to be a part of this reunion. Which was not much.

Sammy looked down at the nail tech Noelle who was diligently using a nail file on his toes. He only now realized that she had been smiling and chattering at him about a new nail certification class that she had recently signed up for, and how she hoped he'd let her try out some of her new designs and techniques on him next time he was in. He nodded at her mindlessly, trying to disappear into the cracks of the chair.

If only they had invisible nail polish, Sammy would be bathing in it.

Pragmatic Dramatic

Here we go. This is it.

Sammy froze, realizing he'd been holding his breath like he was watching a horror movie. He peeked down at the lanyard Bruce had passed him. His stomach did a backflip. One little card. One big verdict. And he had no clue what was coming.

* * *

After the latest Congregation meeting, the BOTs and the GLO leaders had agreed on a sort of truce, at least for this event. Principal Goldblum had once again organized the annual "EHS for Animals" shelter animal volunteer day, where kids from the school could earn community service hours by going out to the shelter to help the staff with their tasks of the day. Enough BOT and GLO kids were planning to attend that it seemed only logical for both clubs to officially sanction it as a formal Congregation event.

The volunteer areas had been broken out into four categories:

Meals: Preparing each animal's meals based on their unique dietary needs and feeding them.

Recreation: Playing with the cats and walking the dogs.

Cleaning: Cleaning kennels and assisting with laundry.

Adoption Event: Hosting an adoption event with the public.

When the students signed up to attend, they could indicate preferences on which categories they were most interested in, but they had no control over what task they would ultimately be assigned to. They would find out their assignments at registration.

Sammy was fine with anything but cleaning. But if he had to bet, the rest of the students probably felt the same, because who in their right mind would choose to go to an animal shelter, do nothing with the actual animals, and instead spend the day cleaning pee-soaked blankets?

Sammy had been worried about being grouped with option number three, Cleaning, for days now. The less students that volunteered to do it, the better the chance he had at being randomly assigned to it.

His anxiety continued to grow as he and his dad bumped down the long shelter driveway that had more holes than the surface of the moon. Finally, the trees parted and the whole scene came into view. Sammy saw students everywhere, buzzing about like bees around a hive. He heard a symphony of dogs barking and kids talking. There were two tables set far apart from each other: one said "Adoption Event" and the other "Registration."

He gave his dad an awkward hug over the armrest and dashed out of the car.

Bruce Bailey was working the registration table. Sammy hadn't realized that Bruce would be here — he hadn't attended the last GLO meeting. Maybe he'd come with his brother Matthew, who *was* there on official GLO business.

Matthew was there as the Prism photographer. Sammy and Indigo had given him the express assignment of getting photos of GLO Club members looking helpful and busy (and hopefully excluding as many BOTs as possible).

Matthew was also forbidden from taking photos of ladies all day. Of course, Sammy and Indigo wouldn't know until they reviewed the pictures after the event if he had actually heeded this rule.

Sammy approached the table and greeted Bruce. Both Bailey brothers were very funny and smart students, but they often let their want to have fun override their best judgment, getting them into trouble sometimes. Matthew was consumed with flirting with the ladies, while Bruce was a quieter version of Matthew, preferring instead to dish out scathing commentary on the world with a comedic sarcasm.

Another difference was that Matthew was much more invested in his work with the GLOs, whereas Bruce just went with the flow.

At all times.

Each of the day's volunteer tasks had been associated with an animal, and the animal on your name tag lanyard determined your shelter assignment for the day.

Turtle = Meal Prep

Dog = Recreation

Rabbit = Kennel Cleaning

Cat = Adoption Event

"Hey, Sam," Bruce calmly offered as a greeting. He began scanning down the participant list while holding a highlighter, focusing his gaze on his guiding finger which was pressed against the paper. He reached Sammy's name and moved his hand to the right on the printed grid to determine which category Sammy had been assigned.

Well? What is it? What IS it? Sammy had never realized how long a simple check-in could take. When something this important is on the line, urgency is key. Bruce's calm, slow, and never-ruffled demeanor was not what this situation called for as far as Sammy was concerned.

Armed with the knowledge of Sammy's fate, Bruce highlighted the entire line, marking Sammy as in attendance. He reached into a box under the table and extended a lanyard to Sammy without a word, holding the verdict in his hands.

He felt like he was going to barf. He couldn't look. And yet he couldn't not.

And just like that, there it was.

Rabbit.

Not surprisingly, probably by manifesting the one thing he didn't want by putting all of his focus on it, Sammy found himself assigned to Kennel Cleaning.

Sammy implored him. "Oh please, Bruce, no, I can't do that. Do I look dressed to clean up diarrhea or spray for fleas?"

He stepped back from the table to show off his stretch pleather pants, blue Golden Girls shirt, white sneakers with the famous iridescent rainbow stripes, and a scarf with assorted animal faces on it. To him, one sight of this outfit would leave Bruce with indisputable proof that Kennel Cleaning was not possible, nor humane, for someone this fashionable. He knew no one else wanted to do it either, but still, Sammy knew he was...special. Different. An exception.

"Uh, I don't make the rules, I just pass these out. I'm not even supposed to be here," Bruce said aloofly. "And in all honesty, I'm not sure you look dressed to do anything with animals, except maybe stroll the *cat*-walk." He smirked, proud of his joke.

While this was no time for jokes, Sammy had to admit that was a good one.

He then noticed Bruce was in a blue shirt.

Sammy and Indigo had advised the GLOs to wear the color blue somewhere prominently in their wardrobe today, to help them stand out from the BOTs. They had assumed that the BOTs would be in their signature red clothing, and they couldn't bear for appearances to imply that there were more BOTs than GLOs in attendance.

To ensure this didn't happen, they had invited Darla and Matthew to come and document the event for the Prism, and they hoped that the article would reflect their own "Blue Ocean" washing out all presence of the "Red Sea." Blue Ocean was the new nickname Sammy had made up in his mind for a swarm of GLO kids, and he was quite proud of it.

He decided to use this time to kiss up a little.

"I see you wore blue. That's awesome, thanks for supporting the GLOs, Bruce!"

"Say what?" Bruce glanced down at his retro Beatles shirt in confusion.

"GLO Club members were told to wear blue today. We talked about it in the last meeting, and I also talked about it in our Squad leadership call that you were in as well... I thought that is why you wore that."

"Matthew told me to wear this shirt, but I didn't ask why. I get it now. Okay, sure. GLO on, brother," he said, holding up his hand for a handshake.

"Uh, GLO on." Sammy smirked and awkwardly shook Bruce's hand. "But listen, before I go, we have to talk." Sammy's dark eyes were now illuminated with determination. "I need you to change my assignment. I simply cannot do Kennel Cleaning. I just can't. Literally."

"Literally? You 'literally' can't clean the kennels?"

Sammy hated intelligence posturing, unless of course he was doing it. He was much more of a "pragmatic dramatic." If something grammatically incorrect would help to make the situation more dramatic, then drama beat grammar.

Every time.

"Whatever," Sammy continued. "The point is, I need you to make the change."

"I'm not allowed to change it, bud. They need a specific amount of people on each task, and if I changed it, they would find out. Plus, I'd be one lanyard short down the line. Sorry."

Sammy looked at Bruce's lanyard, struggling to see what category he had gotten. Bruce lifted his nametag up from behind the table where it was hanging from his neck. "Oh, yeah, check it out, I got 'Dog.' Which is lucky for me because Matthew and I are thinking of getting a dog soon, so it'll be nice to take some on walks and see which one we click with. I want to take that black lab Christopher on a walk first, he looks cool," he said, pointing to one of the cages. Bruce looked the most animated that he has all year.

Truth be told, Sammy's first choice had been the Adoption Event. He liked sales and trying to convince people to do what he wanted them to do, plus he wanted to have the biggest tangible impact of getting these dogs and cats homes *today*.

Also, Sammy was the closest that a young man could get to being a crazy-cat-lady, and having a Cat lanyard would have been icing on the day's cake.

Beggars can't be choosers though, so he could live with walking animals instead.

"How about you and I switch? Let's be honest, you know that you don't want to wrestle hyperactive dogs around the entire neighborhood, and wouldn't staying inside where it is nice and cool be a better option for you?"

The ABCs of Sales: Always Be Closing.

Unfortunately for Sammy, he forgot one tiny detail: Bruce wasn't like the other gullible, easily steered kids that Sammy was used to bending to his will.

"Give me a break, Sam." Bruce changed his inflection to a sarcastic tone, continuing on with a mock conversation between he and Sammy. "*Hey Bruce, wouldn't it be better to clean up crap and urine all day rather than walk nice dogs around on a sunny day?' 'Great point, Sammy, yes! Hey, maybe instead of playing in the soccer game next week, I could clean the porta potties at the field. Yeah, that's a good point, since it is nice and cool in there.*" The sarcasm was dripping off him.

Sammy had hoped to leave the negotiation with nothing lost and everything gained, but he realized that wasn't going to work here. Sammy resigned himself to the knowledge that this was going to require another tactic.

The one thing he knew was that he couldn't be stuck scrubbing kennels all day — not with those pants, not with his dignity on the line. The GLOs were counting on him to represent their best selves, not to smell like a wet mop. If he had to strike a deal to keep that image polished, well... wasn't that leadership?

"Okay, okay, bring it down a few notches," Sammy said to Bruce with a smirk. "How about this. Speaking of soccer, I know that you were wanting to be a starter this season, but Coach Rusty didn't think you were ready. What if I convince him that you are ready and should start next weekend?"

Bruce's permanently tired-looking eyes perked up. "You could do that?"

"I'm the Captain, he always listens to me. I guarantee I could. But you must know that it is up to you to prove yourself after that, I can't keep arguing for you again and again if you whiff your chance. But I can certainly get you that chance to prove yourself."

Sammy could tell this was going to work.

"Now we're getting somewhere," Bruce said, leaning forward. "So, the deal is that I switch lanyards with you, and I spend the day cleaning up *your* dog crap and pee, and you will help me become a starter on the soccer team?"

"Well, it isn't *my* poop and pee, but otherwise, yes. And I can help you be a starter for *one* game. After that you are on your own."

"It might as well be your crap! It certainly isn't mine!" Bruce looked frustrated and disgusted at the thought.

Sammy smiled and nodded, assessing that he had won.

Bruce noticed Sammy's smugness too and realized that this was too easy for Sammy. He decided he could get more out of the deal, because of how clearly desperate Sammy was for this outcome.

"Sounds *pretty* good, but you are asking a lot of me. I mean after all, you are asking me to scrub up poop all day. I could even get fleas from this!" Bruce said overdramatically, playing on what he wisely knew would be a fear of Sammy's. "I have an idea of what would seal the deal for me. You know, I've been wanting the same awesome soccer cleats that you have, but my mom says they are too expensive. If you'll buy me a pair, *plus* make me a starter for a game, I'll shovel your crap."

He stared expressionless at Sammy as a master of negotiation always does. However, in this case, this was simply Bruce's normal expression.

"I don't have that kind of money!" Sammy said. "My parents paid for them. What do you want me to do, steal them?"

"I'm not suggesting crimes of course, but you do what you need to do, just don't tell me." Then, an idea came to him. "Aren't you sitting on a bunch of GLO money? Maybe the club could donate to help a member out?"

Sammy gasped. He did have access to the GLO student accounts that are funded by club participant fees, but he couldn't possibly steal money from the GLOs to bribe Bruce for his own personal gain.

Could he?

"Look, I'm not asking anything big. You used GLO money to help Maryam's refugee thing the other week, and now you are working on making the school buy those stupid dim earth-friendly lightbulbs or whatever. Why can't the club help me? *I'm* in need!" Bruce seemed more convinced of the viability of the scheme by the second.

"I...but...it just seems wrong," Sammy protested, feeling a pull in his gut that this was simply not right. "This can't be a piggy bank that we just pull from any time we want. It has to be for reasons that support our GLO Constitution. I don't think buying you new soccer shoes qualifies as a 'greater good.'"

"Fine then, enjoy shoveling." Bruce pushed a bucket filled with sponges, scrub brushes, and rubber gloves into Sammy's stomach and sat back down smugly.

Sammy glanced over into the kennel's open door and saw several kids on their knees, scrubbing and washing the entryway floor, filing up garbage bags with excess fur that they had pulled from the unvacuumed corners. He gagged a little in his mouth.

"It's a deal," Sammy blurted out, before he could think about what he was saying. It was almost as if the words were said by someone else.

Bruce stood up, and without saying a word, took off his Dog lanyard and handed it to Sammy, took the Rabbit one for himself, and sat back down just as someone else approached the table to check-in. Sammy put the bucket back down on the registration desk, and slowly walked towards the shelter, feeling relieved, yet more burdened than ever.

He could feel that something had shifted in that moment. Something he wasn't sure he could change back. He was going to use funds entrusted to him by his community to personally benefit himself instead of them.

Sammy knew he wasn't typically a crisis-of-conscience sort of fellow, so the fact he felt this way shook him to the core. He felt uneasy. He started to panic.

Should he go back and rescind the deal? Is there time to undo everything?

He looked back to see that Bruce had left the table, and had been replaced by Cici, who was sitting there in her red shirt, smiling and handing out lanyards while pitching BOT membership at every break in a conversation.

Sammy looked back into the shelter and saw Bruce, holding his bucket, being steered off into the long hallway towards the kennels. From inside the shelter, he could faintly hear Miss Filgueira's voice. "Do I have everyone from the Dog group? 1, 2, 3, 4, 5, 6, 7, 8, 9…." She began counting off. "Does anyone know who we are missing? We seem to be missing one student."

She and the other members of the Dog group started to look around. Just then, Ronald looked over his shoulder and caught Sammy's eye as he attempted to hide behind the door.

"Oh, it's Sammy! See, over there, he has a Dog badge on." He pointed over to Sammy, who suddenly felt all eyes on him. "Over here!" Ronald smiled and waved at Sammy, assuming he was lost.

If only he knew how lost Sammy was.

Under Control

"Sammy, we need to talk." Indigo's eyes looked wilder than he had ever seen them before. She was speaking quickly, almost auctioneer-style, chattering away in a stream of consciousness rant.

"I cannot live with what Benjamin did in the Prism! I can't believe they allowed him to personally mock and insult us, you for being fancy, and me for being…what, a hippie? Latina? I can't let him get away with it!"

Sammy agreed with her and knew her frustration was justified. But right now, more than anything, he felt compassion for her as her mind was clearly spinning.

He tried to reduce the temperature. "The guy's a jerk, *you* know that better than anyone! Don't let him get to you. Let's just take the high road and move past this. His opinion means absolutely zero to me anyway."

Sammy could tell Indigo was having a hard time accepting that Benjamin got away with publicly shaming them without any consequences. She kept talking about the litany of reasons she was angry — angry at him, angry at Megan for writing the article, angry at Mr. Miller for allowing it to be printed, and angry that basically everyone knew this type of name-calling was wrong but just seemed to just go along with it because it was easier. What was worse, some people even found Benjamin's insults and rants to be funny. She couldn't begin to understand that, either.

Sammy hoped that he could distract her from allowing the anger to consume her. Ever since receiving Reginald's wedding invitation, Sammy felt as though he had been hit by lightning and awoke from a bad dream. For so many months, he had been consumed with anger and bitterness towards Cleo and the rest of the BOTs. He had been hating, *truly hating*, people he previously liked, and others that he didn't even know. It seemed pretty crazy in hindsight.

He marveled at how this club had changed the way he saw the world, and the other kids at EHS. He had missed so much of Cleo's life, and for what? He was tired of going around with so much hate in his heart. The day that Reginald's wedding envelope arrived, Sammy had vowed then and there: no more.

Unfortunately, Indigo seemed to have taken the reverse path. While she had approached the clubs with more passivity at the start, she now seemed to be consumed by them. She was angrier than Sammy had ever seen her. This lovely, carefree little forest fairy looked at him now with anger and a deep resentment in her eyes. Seeing her this way, he couldn't help but feel guilty for his part in dragging her into this mess.

She asked Sammy to set up a meeting between her and Benjamin at recess today. She had to have some clarity, hopefully an apology, and some contrition on Benjamin's part before she could move on.

Through a series of silly notes passed at lunch, Sammy convinced Benjamin to meet up with Indigo, which wasn't difficult since he knew Benjamin still carried a torch for Indigo deep down. When it came to her, any attention seemed to be good attention as far as Benjamin was concerned. It was written all over his face any time they were together.

The bell shrieked, and Indigo was already waiting by Sammy's locker. Without a word, they fell into step, two soldiers headed for the front lines of recess diplomacy. As they walked outside on the long and nerve-wracking journey to confront the ruins of yet another relationship casualty of the GLOs and BOTs, Sammy reflected on how he had a similar task ahead of him.

Sammy's own mission loomed just as large. He still hadn't talked to Cleo. "Couldn't find the perfect moment" — the phrase alone made him cringe. That was code for *couldn't find the guts*. And guts were exactly what he needed if he didn't want to spend the rest of this year missing his best friend. Pool days, movie nights, holidays still to come — all of it flashing before him like a highlight reel with a ticking clock in the corner.

He slowed near the rock wall. Indigo had her own battle — and Benjamin Rosa was her war. Best to let her fight it solo. He knew that if he was going to achieve his goal of enlightened tolerance, he would need to avoid anything that would ignite the Bozomin-contempt that was permanently bubbling just under the surface. Easiest way to do that — steer clear of the dope at all costs!

Still, it wasn't only moral restraint keeping Sammy quiet. It was distraction. His brain was a pinball machine of panic. How was he going to explain the missing money for Bruce's shoes? The thought clanged around nonstop.

And thanks to Principal Goldblum's new advisory oversight of the clubs, this wasn't just a bad look — it was potential doom. The administration had finally taken note of the growing size and impact that these groups were starting to have at EHS and determined that faculty oversight was required, so Principal Goldblum volunteered. The woman was equal parts Mother Teresa and Judge Judy. She trusted students to "self-govern," but if she ever discovered Sammy's little "donation," she could dissolve the GLOs faster than he could spell "expulsion."

Sammy perched on the wall, pretending to check his phone while watching Indigo and Benjamin hash it out. Arms flailed. Fingers jabbed. Indigo's hair feathers snapped like warning flags in the wind. Their words were low, but the body language was practically screaming.

Then…a plot twist. The yelling softened into laughter. A shove, a grin, a playful shoulder bump. Benjamin even draped an arm over her before she pushed him away, blushing and laughing.

The whole display was making Sammy physically ill.

By the ten-minute mark, the storm had cleared. Indigo gave Benjamin a quick smirk and a light tap on the arm — the kind of gesture that indicated a peace treaty, and perhaps something flirtier than that — and started walking back toward Sammy. He was dying to know every detail. Dying was putting it lightly. It felt like waiting for a cliffhanger to end.

Hurry up, he thought. The suspense might actually kill him before she got here.

"So? I'm dying to hear!" Sammy leaned into Indigo in anticipation of a hush-hush reveal. "How'd it go? What did he say?"

He could tell immediately that something was off. "It was…good. We are good." She picked up her tan, leather fringed purse that she had asked Sammy to hold and started to walk towards the school. This alarmed Sammy, as the bell hadn't even rung yet.

"'Good?' What does that mean?" he asked persistently.

"It means…good. Benjamin and I reached an understanding." She gave a forced smile to Sammy as he hurriedly rushed behind her, trying both to keep up and make sense of this turn of events.

"Um, okay," he said. "Can you tell me anything else?"

"There's nothing else to say, really," she said with a layered tone. "Things should be smoother from here on out."

"Did he at least apologize for what he said about us?"

"Not exactly. He acknowledged it was mean, and maybe wrong, but he isn't sorry about it because he said it worked in getting the BOTs more attention." She entered the school doors just as the bell rang.

"But half of the school hated it! The entire GLO club hates what he is saying, not to mention many of Ronald's Compass Club kids." He continued, "and even Cleo's church friends — they are nice kids and thought it was mean too!"

She rolled her eyes. "He didn't care if they liked it. He just cared if they read it. He feels that any press is good press."

Sammy could relate to that, as that had been his life's motto. Now, knowing that Benjamin endorsed that mindset, completely soured the entire theory. He'd have to rethink his whole approach on life.

Sammy continued to push. "So…nothing was really accomplished, he just acted like a jerk…"

Indigo cut Sammy off. "No, that's wrong. You're right that he can't be reasoned with. But he and I reached an arrangement that we believe will help both clubs to move forward in a mutually beneficial way. We will both get out our messages without having the other group get in our way — no more fighting for the same limited newspaper space!"

Sammy paused to allow her to fill in the blanks, but instead the silence hung out there as heavy as a raincloud.

He finally conceded. "…and the arrangement is?"

The hallway had started to clear out as students moved into their next classrooms. She turned to Sammy and said, "I've got to run, Sammy, but trust me, it's all under control."

As she walked away, her last words echoed through his mind.
Under control.

Under whose control? What is being controlled? He felt a deep unease at what these terms may be.

He knew Benjamin couldn't be trusted. And after the fiasco with Bruce, Sammy knew deep down that even he himself couldn't be trusted.

The question is, could Indigo?

S'il Vous Plaît

Cleo stood in front of the cluttered table, sorting through envelopes and cards and charts that seemed to be piled taller than her. While it looked like a disorganized mess, there was a method to her madness. She took her job of organizing the RSVPs as well as the seating chart for Reginald's wedding very seriously, despite how obvious it was to her that her father was hoping that tasking her with this job would cool her passive aggression towards Viv.

And she hated to admit it, but the plan was kind of working.

Cleo looked forward to coming home and finding the mailbox full of little gold envelopes every day, like a treasure chest full of gold coins just waiting to be claimed. She would sort through the responses, and mark down the respondents' participation, guests, and food choices on a large grid that she had made for the special occasion.

She had also drawn a large seating chart with each of the eight person tables that would be at the event to plan attendees' table assignments. She had traced a coffee can to represent each of the tables on the chart, then she gave each table a letter name, and each seat at each table a number. She would then transfer each attendee's seat assignment back to her RSVP chart for her father to review.

As she was sorting through today's bounty, she started to giggle. In her hand was the response from the Rosa family indicating that all four of them would attend. Next to their meal choices, in Benjamin's messy handwriting, was a scrawled note: *"Let's get Mr. A's love life 'BACK ON TRACK!'"*

She chuckled to herself. Unlike the school, there was no debate that Reginald's love life had been off track. Cleo hadn't made sense of why Viv was the one to finally bring him out of his dating slump, although admittedly she hadn't put much effort into finding out.

She put the RSVP down, feeling a little guilty about the many efforts Viv had made to strengthen their connection. But Cleo had continually rejected her offers: to take her bridesmaid dress shopping, to weigh in on the wedding meal options from the restaurant's tasting menu, the list went on and on. Her father may be marrying Viv, but Cleo had no obligation to like her, she told herself. Now, though, as she settled into the rhythm of seat-charting, she began to allow herself to imagine what it might be like if she allowed herself to settle into this new life, too.

She processed the Rosa RSVP on the attendee chart, and then she walked over to examine the seating chart. She had anticipated the Rosas coming, and had already placed them at Table G, seats 1-4. However, she hadn't figured out yet who would be best to sit with them.

They were a pleasant family, but Benjamin's dad's brash demeanor could be difficult for strangers to warm up to. And to be honest, Benjamin was no walk in the park at times either. Maybe she could sit his mom Didi and his little sister Alice with strangers and give Wyatt and Benjamin a table of their own.

The Rosa girls would probably love the break!

Aside from considering who would want to sit with the Rosas, and knowing how picky the Rosas themselves could be, she had found herself mentally paralyzed trying to find tablemates for them that they too would find suitable.

Cleo knew it should be a married couple who had never been divorced — that topic was a powder keg with the very religious and conservative Wyatt. She also hoped that she could put at least one teen at the table to keep Benjamin occupied and out of trouble. Finally, she was hoping to find people that didn't know them very well so that the Rosas' difficult reputation wouldn't precede them.

Cleo had been avoiding placing anyone at the table with them up to this point, however with only a handful of RSVPs left to receive, it was getting down to the wire. She prayed that an answer would come to her in one of the last few envelopes that were still to arrive before this weekend's deadline.

She ripped open the next envelope and froze. She was in disbelief. Cleo didn't even know that they had been invited, and yet here was their response card.

> NAME: *IRIS FAMILY*
> _X_ WILL *ATTEND*   __WILL NOT *ATTEND*
> NUMBER OF *GUESTS: 3*

Cleo must have stared at the number 3 for at least five minutes. Her mind raced. Not only did she not know that Sammy's family had been invited, but she also had no idea if *Sammy* knew that he had been invited.

Or, that he was coming.

Had his parents filled out the form without Sammy's knowledge? Did he even know her dad had gotten engaged? If he knew, why hadn't he brought it up? Was he mad that she hadn't told him herself? Cleo felt like an insecure little kid, frantically wondering if her friend was mad at her or not.

Maybe this was all on her for not telling Sammy to begin with. She figured that getting an invitation in the mail out of the blue must have been a hard way for him to hear about her father's wedding. That is, if he knew at all.

Back when they were inseparable, they would've talked this whole thing to death by now. The dress, the cake, the woman herself…and oh, how Cleo wished they had. But she hadn't known that Sammy would be invited, so who could blame her?

Sammy could, that's who.

The wedding was only a couple of weeks away, and Cleo's stomach did a flip as she wondered what she'd say to him. Would Sammy be hostile? Would he completely ignore her? Would he even attend at all? She had to be prepared for anything.

As Cleo went over to the seating chart, it felt like she was walking to the guillotine. She knew that the worst-case-scenario was inevitable. Her hand was trembling at what she had to do next.

In Cleo's opinion, most "worst-case-scenarios" were overblown, overly dramatic, unnecessary fears. Things were almost never as bad as anticipated.

But *this* worst-case-scenario was just that.

THE WORST.

And that *still* may have been an understatement. Cleo could think of no worse scenario for her father's wedding than this. And that definitely included the couple breaking up — she saw that as a *best*-case-scenario!

At all other tables, the remaining vacancies were two person openings, meant for couples or friends coming together. There was only one table that had an opening for a three-person family.

Cleo picked up her pen, and with her hand trembling, assigned the Iris family to Table G, seats 6-8. She paused, horrified at what she had just done. Cleo had just placed her explosive former best friend at the table of his bombastic, arrogant archenemy.

Sammy would be sitting with Benjamin at Reginald's wedding.

She knew that the parents would get along, which was half of the battle. Sammy's parents Mac and Alex would meet the basic moral standards of the uber-religious Rosas, but the Irises' more earthy unconventional ways, especially when it came to Sammy's eccentricities, may cause some strife.

She started to consider what Sammy would do when he got to the table.

How would he react? What would he be wearing? Let's be honest, the boy knew how to dress for an occasion.

He usually *was* the occasion.

Cleo groaned. What would Benjamin say about Sammy's outfit? The possibilities got worse and worse as she thought about it. She had to turn off her racing brain.

Then, her mind went to the worst possibility of them all. What if Benjamin exposed the secret and told Sammy about their arrangement with Darla and Megan? She hoped the flimsy pact between herself, Benjamin, Megan, Darla, and Indigo would hold firm.

No one could ever know. And no one did know. Yet.

If Sammy found out, then he would confront Indigo, and she would confront Benjamin about his broken vow of silence, and then Indigo and Sammy would both find out that Cleo was involved, and the repercussions of that were…unspeakable.

Her mind was racing. Her heart was racing. She clutched her hands together in prayer, closed her eyes, and began asking God for guidance. As she pleaded for help in finding a righteous path to best to handle the multiple tragic situations she was facing, something popped into her head.

Cleo had once heard a wise saying that fit perfectly here: *It's always best to prepare for the outcome you desire.* She smiled, right then and there committing to plan for a reconciliation with Sammy, which was undoubtedly the outcome she desired. The rest of it was a worse-case-scenario stuff, and she wouldn't let her mind go there today.

It's never as bad as you think.

Her smile turned to a frown as she realized something else. The sage words in the quote that had just given her such solace, had been taught to her by none other than…Viv! She shuddered, worrying that the same "Viv Virus" that had hijacked Reginald's formerly working brain had just snuck into her own bloodstream as well.

There had to be a pill for that.

Big Score

Sammy turned his face up to the sky, closing his eyes and taking in the warmth of the late afternoon sun. In trying to soak up as much sun as possible, he leaned too far back and lost his balance, catching himself just before he fell off the bench in front of his team, not to mention an entire field of spectators. He quickly stood up and did a few back handsprings and dramatic stretches, acting as if he had intended to nearly pratfall in front of the entire town.

Sammy returned to sit on the bench, looking at the field just in time to see Bruce making an impressive pass so forceful that the kick knocked him on his back, setting Matthew up for an easy tap of the ball into the goal. As the field erupted with cheers, Bruce stood up, pointed to his glistening new shoes, and gave Sammy a thumbs up.

He had been laying it on thick all day, which was really starting to concern Sammy. Bruce was being so obvious, wasn't he worried about getting caught?

Because of Principal Goldblum's seemingly limitless trust in the club members, Sammy was easily able to snag some GLO Club money to pay for Bruce's shoes. When Sammy was turning in the money from the GLO's latest fundraiser, he had taken out the bribe withdrawal — enough to keep Bruce at bay. He didn't know why he felt he even had to deliver on this pact since he could technically turn back on the deal now that the shelter day was over. But Bruce had some scary friends, and Sammy knew that he would either be answering to them, or he would provoke Bruce to turn him in just for the *intent* he had to take the money. He had no choice, he told himself.

He wasn't sure what was true anymore.

He had given the money to Bruce, not even sure if he would follow through on buying the shoes or simply pocket the money for something more "Bruce-y" such as expanding his 60's rock band T-shirt collection. But when he showed up at soccer today, Sammy saw for himself that the shoes had been purchased. He felt some relief in at least knowing where the stolen money went.

But this was also annoying on two counts: First, Sammy no longer held the solo title of most fashionable shoes on the team.

You can mess with a boy's morals, but to mess with his fashion status is a whole new level of offense.

Secondly and more importantly, he couldn't even watch one of their soccer games now without those stupid shoes taunting him. His crime had a permanent spot on the field — and apparently, in his brain too.

"Hey, Coach Rusty!" Sammy yelled down the empty bench. The coach turned his head to Sammy, keeping one eye on the field and one on him.

"Hey, Iris. Whatever it is, can we talk about it later? I'm kind of busy right now as you see!"

A whistle blew, indicating a break in the action.

"Oh yeah, I just wanted to say thanks for letting Bruce take my spot as a starter for this game. He really wanted a chance to prove himself, so I offered my spot out of the kindness of my heart..."

...and the consequences of my embezzlement.

"It's no problem, Iris! The other team is horrible, so this is actually a perfect game for him to be out there. In fact, I think we could win with *only* Bruce on the field. Plus, he's killing it today. Maybe you should get worried!" he said, laughing at the provocation.

Sammy had thought Bruce's excuse about the shoes being the reason he wasn't a top tier player was bogus. However now, after seeing him scoring and passing and head butting in today's game like he never had before, Sammy conceded there could be some truth there. Either way, Bruce was a solid player, but Sammy felt absolutely no threat that this would risk him losing his own status as a team starter or Captain.

Let him have his moment in the sun.

As Vinnie scored another goal, Sammy leaned over to high-five a teammate, any teammate, but no one was there.

Where was everyone?

Sammy had been paying so much attention to the game (and the shoes) that when he turned his head and looked around, he saw that he was the only player still on the bench. He looked to his right and saw a few of the resting players and other standard benchwarmers gathered in a huddle at the end of the bench.

Feeling the need to still play the part of the Team Captain, he walked over to break up what he assumed was a guys-gone-girl-crazy gossip session led by Matthew, to encourage his teammates to refocus and cheer for the players on the field.

When he poked his face into the huddle, he saw what they had been hunched over. It was the newest issue of the Prism. That was odd; it wasn't supposed to be out until tomorrow.

Fellow GLO club member Tommy Lee Friedrick enthusiastically handed Sammy the paper. "Check it out! This is epic! *Every single article* is about us!"

He started hopping around and pointing down the page, highlighting the titles. "Here!" He pointed to the title *Bright Future Ahead with Strong Club Leadership.* "…and here!" *Survey Reveals 70% of Students Most Value Honesty in Leaders.*

"How did you get this?" Sammy asked.

"Darla is my girlfriend, so she gave me a copy early. Don't rat on her, okay?" Tommy Lee implored.

"Oh, I don't care, I just wondered. Your secret's safe with me." Sammy scanned down the paper, his heart filled with joy. Every single article was for or about the GLOs — it was incredible.

Compliments about GLOs, statistics that supported the moral superiority of GLOs, even pieces that promoted GLO membership by featuring highlighted members. Front and center, Sammy saw a big photo of Indigo next to a feature article about her rise to GLO leadership. At first, he felt a pang of jealousy pass through him. But he swallowed it down; if he couldn't be the first GLO to get a member feature, he was glad it was her.

Still, though — as much as Sammy enjoyed demonstrating his capacity for nobility, something didn't add up. He thought back to the cryptic arrangement Indigo had come to with Benjamin the other day at recess. Was it possible that their compromise was somehow behind the feature?

Thankfully, each of these benchwarmers was either a GLO member or unaffiliated, so Sammy didn't have to take any guff from them about how unfair it was that everything in this week's Prism was about the GLOs. He could enjoy this moment unhampered. Sammy realized he didn't have time to read the whole thing now, but he couldn't wait to get his hands on a copy in the morning.

"This is amazing, thanks so much for telling me! But listen…," he turned to the huddled group and continued. "*Do not* mention this to any of the BOT members on the team, okay guys? I can't have them losing focus and not playing their best on the field. Just put this away for now, and we can rub it in their noses at another point."

"You've got it Cap'n," Tommy Lee said with a salute to Sammy, then folded the paper and placed it in his soccer bag.

As Sammy returned to his place on the bench alone, the guys continued to draw attention to themselves, clucking away and high fiving. So much for subtlety.

As the minutes wore on and Sammy was still warming the bench, watching Bruce play endlessly, Sammy's patience for his "good deed bribe" was wearing thin.

He had been on the bench for almost the entire game, which was not at all how he had anticipated the deal. He had figured that Bruce would start the game, play for a few minutes, and *boom*, Sammy would find himself back on the bench so fast he'd have whiplash. Instead, Bruce had played nearly the entire game, leaving Sammy to suffer here in Girl-Crazy-Corner.

He was thrilled that the game was almost over, because unlike the other benchwarmers who enjoyed their time talking and goofing around together, for Sammy, riding the bench was miserable. He had never been in a position where he wasn't the center of the sports action.

As the game ended and the team came towards the bench, Sammy high-fived the players on their win. He went back and started packing up his soccer bag, when suddenly he felt a tap on his shoulder.

"How about these shoes, eh?" Bruce said much too loudly. "They are *amazing!* I can't thank you enough for getting them for me!"

Sammy turned around, incensed. "Are you crazy? Keep your voice down!" he whispered. "You do understand that I stole money to give you an advantage, right? If I get caught, *you* get caught! Now get yourself under control." He started dramatically slamming his water bottle, towel, and sweatshirt into his bag.

"Settle down, bro. I was just saying 'thanks.'" He started to walk away, then came back. "You know, I'd be nicer to me if I were you. Don't ever forget that that I shoveled a bunch of crap for you! You didn't buy these as a favor, it was a thanks you gave me for doing a favor for *you*."

Sammy couldn't muster up words to bridge the gap here, nor did he see value in arguing. He decided for once to just say nothing.

Bruce continued. "And speaking of that, Matthew was hoping that you could help him out a bit too."

Sammy looked up at him. "Help with what? This better not be going where I think it is."

"We got to talking and, well...he heard about our arrangement, and um...he was hoping that you could hook him up with some stuff too."

Sammy's face turned white. "You *must* be joking."

"Nothing big. Maybe another pair of shoes, or a video game? I don't think it matters much. Truth be told, I think he just feels left out. Between our agreement, and then Tommy Lee told him about the arrangement that you club leaders have with Darla and Megan, he just wanted to get in on the action."

"Action? What action?" Sammy paused, replaying the whole sentence in his mind. "Wait, Darla and Megan? What about them?" He could feel his heart beating faster and faster as less things were making less and less sense.

"Come on, man, you don't need to play that game. Your secrets are safe with me." Bruce said.

"Apparently, they aren't!" Sammy shouted, louder than he ever intended to. He glanced around and saw people staring at him. He brought his voice back to a whisper. "Why would you tell Matthew what we did? What part of 'I stole money for you, thus we committed a crime together' is unclear to you?"

"He's my brother, what do you expect? Anyway, as I said, he'll keep quiet. Just throw a little something his way and this all goes away. Okay?" Bruce affectionately bumped Sammy with his elbow. "Besides, we wouldn't want this whole thing leaking to Principal Goldblum, now, would we?" he said casually, walking off with Matthew to the parking lot.

Sammy sat there on the bench, feeling like a mouse caught in a trap. He looked down at the chipped nail polish on his manicured fingers. He noticed that his hands were shaking.

He could hear his parents calling his name, realizing that he was the only kid left at the field. He stared distantly into the Pennsylvania wilderness that surrounded his soccer field, pondering how to get out of this mess, and regretting all that had already occurred. His head was swirling with questions, threats, fear, and consequences.

His mind kept coming back to the loudest question of them all.

What "Darla and Megan arrangement?"

Good "News"

The next day, Sammy was laser focused on figuring out what was going on with all of these "arrangements" that the boys were talking about at the game. But first, he had to make some time to marvel at the best issue of the Prism that had ever been printed.

He went by Principal Goldblum's office and noticed that the newspaper stand was empty. Immediately he was fuming. *How did this happen again?* He was angry and annoyed that he hadn't thought to just take Tommy Lee's copy yesterday instead of giving it back to him.

He planned to go down and talk to Mr. Miller again and give him a piece of his mind.

Supply and demand, people!

Then, he realized that a sold-out paper featuring nothing but GLO Club articles was actually a fantastic problem to have. This was proof that the GLO kids were the answer to EHS's problems, and clearly the entire student body could see that by the fact that all of the papers were taken.

Before cornering Mr. Miller at his journalism workshop, Sammy first stopped at his locker to drop off his coat. Stuffed inside one of the slats of his locker, he noticed a copy of the Prism waiting for him.

Are they delivering these now? Is Benjamin the new EHS paperboy? He laughed at the thought of Benjamin wearing a little pageboy hat pulled over his red mop top of hair, riding a tricycle bike around the halls and tossing papers into each locker.

Sammy looked around the halls and noticed that every locker had a copy of the Prism sticking out of their locker slats. What a fantastic service! Maybe he should put a pin in telling off Mr. Miller. For now.

He looked down and began to admire the entirely GLO-centric paper, bathed in glee as he perused one article after another about his club. This was a dream. He had no idea how Indigo had arranged this, and frankly he didn't care. All he knew was that he was thrilled that the GLO Club had finally received the attention it deserved, and that stupid Bozomin was being put in his place. Sammy hoped that he *finally* understood that his bullying and alpha aggression would not be accepted by the amazing students at EHS.

Suddenly, he noticed Benjamin coming down the hallway, holding his copy of the Prism. He was lumbering along with Vinnie and Louie as always. This was the moment that Sammy had been waiting for. He turned to face Benjamin, leaned back against his locker while crossing his legs to show off his fish scale print leggings. He began fanning himself with the Prism, putting on his best smug face. Suddenly their eyes met, and Benjamin smirked directly at Sammy as he continued by, looking neither concerned, nor bothered a bit.

Sammy stood up from his posturing and watched as Benjamin walked by. Was that not the Prism he was holding? Did he not see what a crushing defeat the BOTs experienced today at the hands of the GLO kids by our entire takeover of this issue?

Sammy strained his neck to confirm that Benjamin was in fact carrying a Prism.

Yes, it was the Prism! While he couldn't read the fine print, he could make out many of the same headlines, same header, same layout. So...why wasn't he upset? Did this have something to do with Indigo?

Sammy became less and less sure of who to trust, because clearly something was going on behind the curtain.

He looked back at his paper and began to scrutinize each article, each word, to see what he could be missing. There *had* to be a reason for Benjamin's Cheshire smile.

There just had to be more to this story.

He decided to go to the source. Sammy marched over to Indigo's locker, but she wasn't there. As he thought about it now, he had hardly seen her at all recently. Was she avoiding him? Was this "arrangement" with Benjamin more than just a truce? Could it be an actual arrangement that compromises the GLO kids?

He fumed at a concocted story that began to form in his mind.

Then again, who was he to be suspicious of the ethics of others? He bribed Bruce and is now being blackmailed by Matthew. What could Indigo or Benjamin do that is worse than that?

Sammy was really starting to resent this new and annoying "having-a-conscience" thing.

"Hey you, Pepper!" He turned around and saw Indigo standing there. "We need to talk."

Sammy's mind began to race. Had she figured out about the stolen money? Maybe big-mouthed-Bruce had spilled the beans. Not to mention, at this very moment Sammy had a signed baseball in his bookbag to bribe Matthew with today.

Sammy had made his mind up that no matter what, he would not steal GLO money again, so he snuck into his baseball-fanatic father's room and stole a signed baseball to give to Matthew. Sammy had no idea who Don Mattingly was, or if Matthew liked him, but he figured that alpha-boy athletes like Matthew would probably like that kind of thing.

Next, he'd have to figure out how to explain the missing ball to his dad.

"Helloooo?" Indigo waved her hand in front of Sammy's face. "Is anyone home? You haven't said a word!"

"Oh, sorry, I just have a lot on my mind. What's up?" He attempted to act nonchalant.

Indigo looked at him intensely. "I have been feeling really guilty, because we normally tell each other everything. I think it's time that the truth comes out. We can't have big secrets like this between us. We are leaders of the same club, and if one of us goes down, both of us do, so we have to be on the same page." She looked concerned.

Sammy was panicked. She clearly knows! Would she report him before he had a chance to explain himself? Would she stick by him, or do everything she could to distance herself from him?

The panic was gripping Sammy, and he didn't have a good poker face. Once again, an awkward amount of time passed without him uttering a word.

Indigo hit her limit. "Good talk." She rolled her eyes. "Please just meet me at the rock wall at the beginning of recess. We need to talk. It is *very* important." With that, Indigo started to leave. She was so aggravated that she unknowingly turned her head with such force that her hair feathers hit Sammy in the face as she walked away.

He started spitting and pulling tiny feather strands from his mouth. She turned back. "What did you say?"

"Nothing, it's just that..." he paused, seeing that she was in no mood for him to reprimand her about her feathers. "Nothing. See you at recess."

Sammy watched her as she disappeared down the hallway.

This was all too much.

What was he going to say to her? He didn't even know her that well. Could he trust her? Should he tell the truth and get her help, or was he on his own? He could get kicked out of school...or worse. Maybe even arrested! Was having someone else clean those kennels worth all of this?

He flashed back to seeing those kids on their hands and knees, scrubbing floors and picking up urine-soaked fur from the corners of the shelter entryway. Again, he gagged in his mouth a little.

It probably was.

He began walking aimlessly down the hallway. As he passed Mr. Miller's journalism classroom, he looked inside to catch a quick glimpse of the magical old machines in the hopes that the make-shift Santa's workshop would cheer him up. As he squinted his eyes to look, he realized that his view of the machines was blocked by Ronald, who was standing in the room talking to Mr. Miller.

Curiosity overtook him, and he snuck over to the door to listen. He stood with his back against the wall outside the open door, perfectly hidden but with great acoustics to hear what was going on.

"…I just don't understand how it is fair for them to get an *entire* news issue dedicated to their club. There are so many more important things going on here at EHS besides them. It is the Prism's obligation to present all viewpoints, not just one! What happened to freedom of the press?" Ronald's normally calm, measured way of talking was more urgent now.

What a traitor! Just because he can't get any support for his ridiculous Compass Club doesn't mean the has the right to harm the other more successful clubs. Who cares about "freedom of the press" anyway? Give the people what they want, and what they want is GLO! Sammy smiled self-righteously to himself.

Mr. Miller examined the paper that Ronald handed to him. "This is the first time I'm seeing this Ronald, and I thank you for bringing it to my attention. As you know, I give my newspaper staff the right to prepare the publications largely on their own, because I want them to have a sense of autonomy which will help them to prepare for their futures. I can see how this would be frustrating for you since your club isn't mentioned here at all. But in their defense, neither is the other large club, whatever they are called."

Sammy giggled to himself, pleased that Mr. Miller forgot all about the BOT club.

Ronald started complaining, more to himself than directly at Mr. Miller. "How can we reward his behavior? He thinks he can run *everything* at this school. He would gladly take the jobs of the teachers and administrators if he had the chance!"

Sammy's smile fell. Why would Ronald talk about him like that? He had tolerated him when no one else would. Now he was glad he never pitied him enough to join Compass anyway. Sammy was becoming increasingly enraged.

Mr. Miller put his hand on Ronald's shoulder. "Mr. Ross, we shouldn't talk about our fellow students in that way. I understand that he can be challenging sometimes, but he means well and is an overall good person. Even if he is very brash at times!" He chuckled to himself.

Sammy wasn't sure if he should be offended or flattered at Mr. Miller's words.

"So that's it?" Ronald said, deflated.

"I'll tell you what, Mr. Ross, I'll talk to my team and find out why they made the editorial decision to only feature the BOT club in this issue of the Prism. I'm sure they plan to do more diverse features in the future of other groups and goings-on here at the school, don't worry."

Sammy laughed to himself. He means the GLO Club. They were the only ones featured in the paper, not the BOTs. Silly old guy.

Mr. Miller continued. "Actually, all of this aside, I have to say, I've been quite thrilled with the increased engagement with the paper in recent weeks. Going through the entire supply of papers week after week, even needing to print more, has been amazing for us. In fact," he moved closer to Ronald, lowering his voice, "I'll tell you a secret."

Sammy leaned in, nearly falling into the door frame, exposing his nibby-nosing.

"The school has been threatening to get rid of the journalism program for years here at EHS. As you know, schools are making the horrendous move towards an elimination of the arts as part of budget cuts, and journalism isn't far from being on that same chopping block."

He sat down, looking defeated. He took off his glasses and massaged the bridge of his nose, closing his eyes momentarily.

"Journalism is something that costs a lot of money, relatively speaking, when you consider the printing of the paper, ink, supplies, high tech and antique machine purchases and upkeep, cameras, film, dark room supplies, the list goes on and on. I have been fighting for years to keep journalism in the curriculum, as I think it is such a fundamental part of education, as well as our democracy. These are huge tentpoles of our society."

He began counting them off on his fingers. "Freedom of speech. Freedom of the press. Freedom of religion. Right to petition the government. And the right to assemble. The First Amendment protects all of these, though in practice, they risk getting lost in the change that is happening to make the news about money. This is why I'm fighting so hard to keep journalism in the curriculum. The creation of these clubs has been a great support for my case that students want the Prism to continue on. I'm hopeful this uptick in interest helps me to keep it on the books here, at least for a few more years."

This story softened Sammy a bit. The same couldn't be said for Ronald.

"Fine." Ronald was less than satisfied. "But can you please also talk to Benjamin about his behavior? Someone must put him in his place! He has been telling everyone that I closed the Compass Club, but I didn't. Now he gets a full issue about the BOTs? I don't see that as a coincidence. It's like he's pulling all the levers at EHS!"

Sammy was frozen, more confused than ever. Both of them were saying this issue is only about the BOTs. They must both be confused.

Was that likely? Probably not. But Sammy had seen the Prism, and it was an all-GLO newspaper. He didn't get it.

Sammy closed his eyes and took a deep breath, trying to calm himself down so he could focus on putting these puzzle pieces together.

Now Ronald is complaining about Benjamin...could Benjamin have been the "he" that they were talking about before? Does that mean it is Benjamin that Mr. Miller finds to be annoying and brash?

He paused, aghast. Does that mean that Mr. Miller forgot the name of the GLO club?

Sammy felt like he was living in an alternate reality. He stared down at the paper that he was holding in his hands and looking back at him was Indigo on the cover of the paper, surrounded by GLO articles from top to bottom. He tried to peek through the crack of the open-door frame to see if he could examine the paper they were holding, but he couldn't make out any details.

Nothing here made sense. That seemed to be a theme around EHS lately.

What was going on?? He couldn't get to recess fast enough to find out.

VIRTUAL REALITY

You ever have one of those moments when everything starts to fall apart — and you can't help but wonder when, exactly, it all went wrong? What single choice sent the whole thing crashing down?

What was the point of no return?

You could say Sammy's moment was the bribe with Bruce.

But you'd be wrong.

The real breaking point started at recess that day — with Indigo. What she told him lit the fuse, and what came after...well, let's just say once the first domino tipped, there was no stopping the chain reaction.

What followed would change everything. And it would change Sammy — completely.

After that recess, he'd never be the same again.

*   *   *

He met Indigo at the rock wall as she requested. Sammy interrogated her as to what was going on. He told her about his spy mission at Mr. Miller's doorway, and the conversation he had eavesdropped on, along with all the questions that Ronald had asked regarding the BOT-exclusive issue of the paper. He told her about Ronald's attempts to figure out a way to stop Benjamin's dominance at the school, and his intense focus on reducing the hold that the GLOs and BOTs have on the news and the administration as a whole.

Sammy questioned her about this skewed reality. He asked her how he was looking at a GLO-centric paper, and yet Ronald and Mr. Miller were discussing a BOT-centric one.

"What is going on?" he demanded. She sat silently with an almost blank look to her face.

Sammy had been going off for what felt like forever — ranting, accusing, throwing every half-baked theory he could come up with at Indigo. She just sat there, quiet, barely blinking, like she was waiting for a storm to pass. The longer she stayed silent, the louder he got, trying to get some kind of reaction out of her. But she wasn't biting.

It finally hit him that she was letting him wear himself out — giving him the space to burn through his emotions before she dropped whatever truth bomb she was holding. The way she looked at him, calm and steady, almost made him angrier. Like she'd already decided he couldn't handle the truth but was going to tell him anyway, just to shut him up before he ran around the school playing detective.

Without a word, she reached up above her head and motioned for Benjamin to come over and join them. Sammy curiously looked behind him to see who she was beckoning. The minute he realized it was Benjamin, the blood drained out of his face. This felt like a trap.

He turned to Indigo. "What are you…"

Benjamin's yell cut him off. "Cleo!" He motioned for her to join them as well.

As they both approached, Sammy felt like a boat in the middle of the ocean, with submarine missiles coming directly at him from all angles. There was no escape. The confrontation was happening, and it was happening right now.

And then, the true tale began to reveal itself.

Benjamin handed Sammy a Prism paper. "Here, take a look at this."

He looked down, barely skimming it. "I know, I've already seen..." he stopped in his tracks. He couldn't believe his eyes.

The paper Benjamin handed him was a completely BOT-centric paper. Where Indigo's face had been, he now saw Benjamin's red mop top smugly smiling back at him. The logo was the same. The layout was the same. Every single title was the same. But the content below each of the titles was 100% different.

He examined the article titled *Survey Reveals 70% of Students Most Value Honesty in Leaders*. The GLO version, which he had nearly memorized, gave accolades to the honest and moral way that their group of light and love operated, without the so-called poisonous and antagonistic messaging of Benjamin and his BOT Brigade.

As he examined the BOT version of the same article, it spoke of the strength and honesty that Benjamin's straight-talk messages gave the student body, cutting through the "fluffy noise" of ineffective groups like the GLO club and its Squad, to ensure the student body was stable and protected.

He couldn't believe what he was seeing. In every article, in every feature, the headlines were the same, but the content below was completely different.

Sammy hadn't spoken since Benjamin handed this to him. He realized now that Benjamin and Indigo had been chattering on, attempting to explain and justify things to Sammy, but he hadn't heard a word.

His eyes and ears started to come into focus as he looked up, fixing his gaze directly at Cleo. Her eyes were glued to the grass, in a mix of shame and guilt.

"I haven't heard...uh, what?" Sammy stared blankly at them, hoping for someone to start over and say something that made any kind of sense.

He turned to his oldest friend for help. "Cleo? What's going on?"

She never looked up from her shoes, resembling a child that had been caught drawing all over their parents' walls in permanent marker. She looked like she wanted to disappear.

"Cleo? Somebody, please explain what is going on." Sammy stood there, facing the BOT paper he was holding, but with his eyes completely out of focus.

Benjamin and Indigo exchanged glances, realizing that their rambling had fallen on deaf ears. This time, they decided to be more direct in their messaging, as they had built up some bravery after having recited the tale once already.

This is the moment that Sammy finally heard the reveal of their "arrangement."

Indigo took the lead. "Well, okay, so do you remember when Benny and I were talking at recess the other week? We were talking about how much effort and energy it was taking to constantly fight each other to get our clubs the most attention at school, both with the students and in the Prism. It was getting impossible to ensure we both got a fair amount of press. So, then we thought, what if we could create *two* versions of the paper? A BOT version, and a GLO version."

Sammy was confused. "What? How could you even…"

Benjamin took over. "It was surprisingly simple. We bribed Darla and Megan…"

"*Convinced*!" Indigo interrupted.

"Sorry, 'convinced' Darla and Megan to write polar opposite articles each week, with Darla's articles totally favoring the GLOs, and Megan's completely favoring the BOTs. They kept the titles the same so that neither the students, nor Old Man Miller would notice the difference. It is *brilliant*!" Benjamin couldn't hold back his excitement about the idea, laughing and clapping like he just scored a goal.

Sammy cut in. "So, your solution to the GLO and BOT fighting was to create completely different realities for the two halves of the student body?" That seemed extreme, even to Sammy.

Benjamin continued to beam. "Brilliant, right?"

Sammy felt like he was in the Twilight Zone. "Indigo, how did he get you to go along with this?" Sammy had been twisting and squeezing his BOT paper so tightly that his hands were completely black.

She grasped Sammy' hand to prepare him for her yet-to-be-delivered news. "It wasn't just Benjamin's idea, Pep. It was mine too."

"But how would the students not find out? I mean, once they grab a paper, if they see the wrong one, they would understand the whole scheme, right?"

Benjamin shook his head. "Where did you get your paper from today?"

"From the front offi..." Wait, no. He remembered it was in his locker.

"In your locker, *exactly*." Benjamin smirked. "See, Indigo and I divided up the student body in two parts, identifying everyone by their 'most likely' club affiliation. GLO or BOT. And for those that are already in a club, even better! Less work for us. We used this to figure out which version of the news they would be given. Then, Megan and Darla were each given a list of their club's distribution list, and they hand-delivered their papers to the appropriate students' lockers. This way, no one will ever know that we are presenting different versions of reality, for lack of a better description."

"No one *will ever* know? You aren't planning to do this again, are you?" Sammy asked incredulously.

"Are you kidding me? Heck yes, we will! This is Jedi-mind-trick sort of stuff here. It is perfect! Every student *thinks* they are reading the same news, the same statistics, and the same events. But in reality, the papers are presenting completely different spins on the information."

Indigo continued. "And what's nice, Sammy, is that things will be so much more convenient for the students. Think about it, now they only have to read curated news just for them, focusing only on what they want to hear. We're doing them a favor, really. They only have to read what they want. Who should have to read anything they don't want to hear? I don't want to hear insulting things about myself or the things I believe in. Do you? This way, they feel great about themselves, and about their club!" Indigo's eyes were glowing as she was pitching.

Sammy couldn't tell if she believed what she was saying, or if she was trying with all of her might to sell him on the idea. Or even herself.

"Oh, and I forgot about this!" she continued. "Making things even *easier,* this news, which is specially pulled together for them, giving them just what they want...then simply *appears* in their lockers unsolicited! They will be so happy, they won't even care *how* it is happening, they'll just be happy that it is!"

Sammy fought back. "Indigo! Are you getting that this will break up the entire school? People are going to get so confused, that they will think that these realities...are actually *real*!"

Benjamin and Indigo conceded that it was likely this would cause a schism in the student body eventually, especially as the students became increasingly confused and frustrated at the other half of the students, wondering how they could support stances that were so different from theirs. The truth didn't stand a chance — not when the students were being pulled and twisted into two completely different realities.

But Benjamin and Indigo figured that this was a concern for another day.

Again…or still…Sammy was speechless. He couldn't understand how they'd fooled themselves into thinking this was a good idea. He knew he wasn't perfect, far from it, but Bruce's pair of shoes seemed to be fairly minor compared to this.

What have these clubs turned everyone into? Stealing from each other? Robbing them of their sense of reality? Pitting friend against friend?

For the first time, he looked up and locked eyes with Benjamin, then Indigo.

Ah, Benjamin and Indigo. He had always wondered what they ever had in common, what may have been the tether to bring such different personalities together as a former couple. But seeing them now, standing side by side, it all looked a little different to Sammy. Maybe a little clearer. Maybe a little messier.

They both wanted to help, he guessed — but only as much as it advanced their own personal goals. Whether anyone got hurt along the way didn't seem to matter as much as getting what they wanted.

Benjamin's goals were obvious. He supported the causes that made sense to him, and to the people who thought like him. He wasn't trying to shut anyone out — it just usually didn't occur to him to look past his own point of view.

Indigo wanted to help *everyone*. But underneath it all, Sammy could see it now — she also wanted to be *seen* helping, to be the one people looked up to. Her good intentions often got tangled up in her need to feel important.

The worst part for Sammy was knowing he wasn't really any better. He'd like to think he'd never play the game the way they did, but deep down he knew he already had. Maybe the only difference between him and them was that they had stopped pretending otherwise. Sammy's stomach twisted as he took in the scene. The clubs had started out as something to unite people — but looking around now, all he could see were the cracks they'd left behind.

And Cleo.

He couldn't stop staring at her. She didn't look shocked. How could she stand there like this was all fine?

"Do you have any questions for us, Sammy?" Indigo stood here, looking as angelic as ever. However, Sammy couldn't help but see things very differently now.

"Uh, YEAH, I'd say so. How long were you planning to keep this up?"

"'How long *were* we planning to keep it up?' This isn't over. This is the way it is now, Sammy, so you better get on board." Benjamin talked with the soft touch of sandpaper, as always.

Indigo stepped in and softly touched Sammy's back, hoping to create a gentler connection. "What he means to say is that this arrangement is best for everyone involved. It is our responsibility as leaders to guide the rest of the students at EHS to help them see things as we see them. We know what's best for them, and they need us to help mold messaging that creates the best experience for them. Can you understand that?"

Sammy couldn't believe his ears. How could they keep doubling down on this? How could they justify how they are manipulating everyone?

He continued with his line of questioning. "So…how did you convince Darla and Megan to do this? They could rat you out at any minute!" He looked back and forth at Indigo and Benjamin, who both, for the first time since this conversation started, seemed apprehensive to speak. "Hello? Anyone? Just fess up, I'm going to find out anyway."

Benjamin spoke. "Cleo, would you like to take this one?"

Sammy's glare settled on Cleo's soulful, dark eyes for the first time in months. He realized in that moment — he had not looked directly in her eyes since the day this all started. The old saying felt very true right now, because her eyes felt like the windows to her soul.

He could see in that look that she was broken. He knew she saw that in him too. He was filled with love, and regret, and a sense of home, all at once as he looked into these warmly familiar eyes.

He hoped that what she said next wouldn't change that.

"Cleo? Just tell him." Indigo looked to be a cross between annoyed and nervous.

Cleo opened her mouth to speak, but nothing came out. Then suddenly, she burst into tears. Indigo rubbed her back, encouraging her to get it over with.

Speaking through the rush of emotions, Cleo began to utter the sordid story.

"I paid them. I went into the club lock boxes in Principal Goldblum's office, and I took money from the BOT fund. Then, Indigo gave me the combination to the GLO fund box, and I took money from there too. I used that money to pay Darla and Megan to write the stories for us."

She paused to catch her breath, as she was nearly hyperventilating.

"After the articles were done, Mr. Miller almost caught Darla and Megan and exposed the whole thing. They started freaking out about how they could lose their jobs if he found out. At that point they said that we need to keep paying them to keep quiet and continue doing this, or they will expose us, telling the whole school what we did."

Sammy paused, trying to digest the entire sordid story. "But they would be telling on themselves if they do that. That'd be stupid," he said.

"Not really. They said they would cover for themselves by claiming that they took the money as part of an undercover exposé story to catch us in the act of using club funds as bribes. So, like Benjamin said, we have to keep up this arrangement or we will all go down for it."

Cleo looked like she aged 10 years in that confession.

Benjamin chuckled to himself. "Whoa, Cleo, let me clear up one point there. If things go wrong, *you* will be the one to go down, not us. You are the one who technically bribed Darla and Megan, and while they may have suspicions, they have no proof that anyone but you stole money and paid them. Sorry, but that's the truth."

Cleo looked at him with more disgust than Sammy had ever seen her peaceful face show before. "Are you *kidding* me? You are the one who made me do this! You said you would blame me for everything if I *didn't* do this, now you are threatening to do the same thing because I *did* do it? I thought we had a deal! You JERK!"

Sammy's eyes bugged out of his head. He had *never* seen Cleo this angry.

Ever.

She continued. "It is your word vs. mine, who's to say anyone would believe you?"

"I mean, we know that the school security cameras would easily show you going in to steal the money. Not to mention, I may or may not have told Kwame to document you being there. Remember when he made you sign in that day?" Benjamin smirked with all the pride of a cat that caught a mouse, but instead of killing it, chooses to torture it for a while just for fun.

This was all too much for Sammy to digest at once. He was flooded with emotions of betrayal, confusion, disgust, anger, and even pity for Cleo and the mess she had gotten herself into.

Then, his old friend "Guilt" returned again, haunting him for the secrets he still held. These clubs had destroyed them, and the only people that seemed to benefit were Indigo and Benjamin.

Sammy had to figure out what to do next.

First, he had to consider self-preservation. If he reported the whole thing, he may be able to escape personal prosecution, because he had been truly ignorant of the whole Prism scheme. However, his hands were *not* clean, as the Bruce and Matthew bribes were still lingering out there. He was pretty confident that they wouldn't tell on him as there would be no way to do so without implicating themselves as well.

Also, if Indigo and Benjamin's plan leaked, Principal Goldblum would immediately begin examining the ledgers, and surely, she would find Sammy's money crimes right there in black and white. This just wasn't an option.

Then there was the moral angle. If he allowed this to continue, he would be permitting the destruction of the student body from within, through a campaign of misinformation and manipulation orchestrated by these two groups whose only motivation was to maintain their powerful roles and their own self-interests. He felt an obligation to do something to stop this, but he wasn't sure how to stop a runaway train like this by himself. The entire structure felt too big to change.

Then…there was Cleo. If he did decide to report this for either of the other reasons, Cleo would be implicated for sure. There would be no escape for her. He could tell by looking at her tear-stained cheeks that she was simply a pawn in this, like the rest of the student body, and, as much as he hated to admit it, a pawn like he was too. Looking at her now, he couldn't justify getting her into trouble. She didn't intend for the harm that she caused. She had done wrong, yes, but she was a pawn in a game being played by much stealthier opponents.

"We can trust you, right Sammy?" He could feel Benjamin's stare burning a hole into the top of his head as he stared at the ground. After a long pause, Sammy nodded silently. Benjamin continued. "That's a good soldier right there."

He brushed it off, acting completely unfazed by Cleo's or Sammy's emotions, too busy stuffing down his own feelings so he could stay focused on victory over vulnerability.

"Now, we need to figure out what to do about Ronald. He must be stopped. That guy won't just give it a rest! We need to eliminate him before he exposes what has happened here. Even if the four of us keep our mouths shut, there are still quite a few loose ends that put each of us, and our clubs, at serious risk. Ronald is a threat here, and we need to put a muzzle on him and his pointless and annoying club. Any ideas?"

No one spoke. The silence was deafening. Then, Benjamin's face lit up. "I have an idea!" He turned his head. "Sammy, I'm looking at you."

Sammy raised his weary eyes, glaring at Benjamin, feeling as though he was too weak to effectively fend off another attack. He was beaten. He was broken. His faith in all that was good in the world was gone. "What," he said, more as a statement than a question.

"You need to frame Ronald for this. You need to go into Principal Goldblum's office and change the ledger to reflect that Cleo's money withdrawals were illegally done by Ronald for the Compass Club."

Benjamin paused to consider the details. He was always very strong in tossing out big ideas, but he had never been the guy to figure out the "how" of his schemes. But he rambled on.

"So, we will make up a story that we shared our lockbox passwords with Ronald or kept them in a notepad that he found or something, we can work out the details later. But you have to go in there and frame him for the missing money. I'll make sure that Kwame leaves the office so that you don't need to sign in, and he can turn off the cameras to Principal G's office from his computer before he leaves. It'll be perfect."

There was that Cheshire smile again.

Sammy and Cleo stood there, speechless at what was being proposed. Framing an innocent kid for their crimes was a shocking moral decline that neither were ready to face. Benjamin appeared completely unaffected as he continued.

"Look guys, wake up. Even if we keep our mouths shut, at some point the money will be found to be missing. This way we get ahead of it." He looked proud of this quick-thinking scheme.

Indigo had been conspicuously quiet throughout Benjamin's proposal. Sammy had assumed she had been disgusted into silence just as he was. Suddenly, she spoke. Her words added shock to awe.

"I think he's right," she said quietly, her eyes filling with tears. She looked only at Sammy, somehow imploring him to agree with her. "The more I think about it, I know it feels wrong, but it is the only way for us to protect ourselves. If we don't do this, all four of us risk being kicked out of school, and having our clubs shut down altogether! We are doing *important* work here, and I couldn't live with losing all of that. No one will care that Ronald or the Compass Club is gone, and this works better for us, because we can recruit those kids into GLO or BOT membership. They will find a home with one of us! Either way, keeping our clubs healthy and protected is what we need to do."

It was Sammy's turn to speak now. He formed his words slowly and emphatically with no efforts to hide his disdain, except for the hushed voice that he had to maintain to keep his yelling discreet.

"Are you both out of your minds!? I'm *not* framing Ronald! He's a good kid. Annoying for sure, but harmless."

"You hate that guy!" Benjamin said brashly.

"I don't hate him. He annoys me with how stupidly hard he tries to make everyone get along, and he just won't realize that it is impossible. He may be a sucker, I'll give you that, but he doesn't deserve this." Sammy paused, pondering another piece of the situation. "By the way, why are you trying to make *me* do this? You do it if you want to!"

Benjamin retorted quickly. "You are the only one in the group who wasn't involved with the Prism situation. So, we need you to do this so that we can be sure that you will keep quiet. With you as a part of the crime, you won't be able to report us."

"I see how that helps you. But why would I willingly get myself wrapped up in this? What could you possibly do to convince me to do such a thing?"

Benjamin smiled, a twisted and crooked Grinch-like smile that expressed a mix of glee and hatred all wrapped up in a bow and aimed directly at Sammy. Then, he said the words that would kick over the domino.

"Well, why don't we ask Bruce and Matthew about that."

Indigo and Cleo both toggled their glances between Sammy and Benjamin, neither one understanding the knowledge that was now implicit between the two boys.

Indigo prodded, "What do you mean, Bruce and..."

Benjamin cut her off, forcing a laugh. "Oh, it's just an inside joke from the soccer team. *Right*, Sammy?"

Indigo and Cleo looked at Sammy for validation. He didn't say a word.

"Is that true, Sammy?" Cleo softly asked with a mix of concern for her friend and confusion at the situation.

Sammy could barely speak. "Yep. It's a riot," he said, staring darts at Benjamin, his face now completely devoid of emotion.

"Then it's settled!" Benjamin said with a glib clap right as the bell rang, signaling the end of recess. "I'll set everything up with Kwame and get back to you. We will plan to do this on Monday when Principal Goldblum goes to lunch. I'll be in touch."

He walked casually away from the rock wall, leaving the others deep in their own thoughts. Sammy knew that recess was over, but he couldn't go back to class. He couldn't sit there and pretend that none of this happened. He turned from the group and ran as fast as he could towards the woods that lined the school's property line, trying to find a place to hide. He didn't realize that what he was looking for was an emotional shelter to hide in, not a physical one.

For now, sitting under the canopy of trees that sheltered him from the drizzle that was just beginning to fall from the darkening skies would have to do.

AT RECESS

Ronald was aghast as he walked into Mr. Miller's workshop to head up the weekly meeting of the Compass Club, which met there every Friday after school. As he scanned the room, he couldn't believe how many people were there. While his normal meetings had about 5-7 people in attendance at most, he walked in now to find nearly 25 students sitting at desks, tables, and turned-around computer chairs, filling up the room in a way that he could only have dreamed. A huge smile spread across his face.

"Wow, word is finally catching on! I knew there were more students who wanted to be a part of our Compass revolution. Welcome everyone!" His voice was buoyant as he smiled and put down his notebooks. "I definitely don't have enough agendas today, but you can share these with your neighbor." He began to pass the sheets around. "For those that don't know, I'm Ronald Ross and I'm the President of the Compass Club. Today I wanted to open up the discussion to get your thoughts on…"

He was cut off by the Compass Club's second-in-command, Chakra Patel. "Ronald, as you can see, we have some guests today who have informed me that they are here to discuss some grievances they have with the BOT and GLO clubs, and they may also be interested in considering joining the Compass Club going forward."

While attempting to act as if this was all very standard, to a keen observer, Chakra's face was bursting with excitement at the potential new growth of their centrist club.

"Fantastic!" Ronald said. "Please, who wants to go first? The floor is yours."

He stood there at the front of the class as one student after another stood up to outline their issue with the BOTs, or GLOs, or both. Some were frustrated that they had no idea what their membership fees had been used for. Some were angry that they felt the clubs were too exclusionary, or too extreme, or forced them to choose between keeping or dumping their long-time friends. Some spoke of hearing rumors that their money had been used to pay for bribes, coverups, or favors.

Ronald, always trying to be fair and find common ground, asked them if they had brought up these concerns in their respective club meetings. But members of both groups said that the regularity of weekly club meetings had waned off, and there only seemed to be meetings an average of once a month now, yet neither club lapsed in collecting their regular club dues. The members weren't sure what they were even paying for anymore.

Chakra asked them what the GLO and BOT leadership, the Squad and Brigade, had been doing instead of member meetings, trying to give them the benefit of the doubt. Perhaps they were preparing or laying groundwork for future club initiatives, she proposed.

Instead, the student members reported that they were always seen at recess huddled on their own, as if they didn't have a care in the world.

A surprising face stood above the rest to take the leadership reins for the opposition. Cici Bubber.

"We paid good money to those clubs because we were told that members got benefits, and now it's obvious that we were just suckers that fell for their lies. We were hustled! They promised us weekly meetings, monthly events, lots of extracurricular get-togethers, and the clubs advocating on our behalf. But we haven't had a true BOT event in months that wasn't just listening to Benjamin blather on about himself. Any event that we have had has been organized by me or Cleo! I heard the same thing about the GLOs too, that after the membership grew, the leaders didn't give a crap about following through for the members."

Shouts and claps of agreement filled the room.

"Same here! The GLOs have been doing a lot of talking, and promising, and painting pretty pictures, but other than a couple of volunteer events ages ago, nothing has happened. Even at those events, it seemed the GLO leaders were more concerned about taking photos and getting good press from their deeds than they were about truly doing good work. *None* of the initiatives that were part of the club's mission statement have happened. I'm honestly not even sure what the GLO Club stands for at this point." After speaking, Autumn sat down next to Maryam who was also clearly frustrated.

This collective group, made up of disgruntled members from both the BOTs and the GLOs, had first met each other during the Congregation meeting. As they talked after the meeting, they were shocked to find out that they had a great deal in common. Each club had painted the opposite club's members in such a villainous way, that they had been pleasantly surprised to find out how similar they were. This was the first red flag for many of them, which was worsened by ongoing conversations between the members who had begun to string together similar problems and concerns happening in both clubs.

"I think I speak for everyone here by saying that we don't feel comfortable going to the GLO and BOT faculty advisor, who also happens to be Principal Goldblum. We can't bother someone as important as her with these issues, so we figured we would take it to the streets." Cici turned to Ronald with a burning intensity in her eye. "We wanted to see if you will actually follow through on your promises, unlike the others."

Ronald listened intently as the students continued to outline their concerns, however he wasn't sure how to help them. Of course, he wanted them to join the Compass Club, but he wanted them to join because they *believed* in middle-ground and common-sense solutions, not just as some form of revenge to the clubs that they had rebuffed.

He didn't feel it was appropriate for him to report these offenses of the clubs, because they were technically private groups that in theory could operate as they chose. Also, most of these accusations were hearsay and could not be proven.

Perhaps by design.

When the passionate dialogue died down, Ronald stood back up from the desk he had rested on as the flood of feedback had poured in. "First of all, I want to say thank you for everything that you have shared with us. We are so appreciative that you have entrusted us with this information, and you have my word that we will keep it confidential. While I don't have the power to reprimand the GLO or BOT clubs, I can invite you to join the Compass Club. We meet every week, *without fail*, and we work diligently to tackle the issues that matter to each of you. *You* say where your money goes. *You* get a say in the causes that the Compass Club supports. Your voice *will* be heard."

He smiled, hoping for accolades, even applause perhaps, but he was met only with apathetic silence.

"I have already paid the GLOs so I'm not looking to join another club. I want someone to help me get my money back or force them to do their jobs!" yelled a boy from the back.

Ronald continued. "If you don't mind me asking, why is it that you are so attached to being a part of one of just these two clubs? They are louder, and more well known, sure. But there are more of us that are part of the Compass Club, or not part of any club at all, than those who are part of either the GLOs or BOTs. *We* are actually the majority! Why not make it official? Join us and let's grow Compass to whole new levels!" He smiled, hoping this time he had gotten through to them.

The apathy continued.

He tried one last time. "Okay well I'll say this. I am so happy that you all chose to come today. I share your shock and frustration that you were misled by the GLOs or BOTs and aren't getting much if anything for your money. All I can do is invite you to invest your future time, effort, and money into joining me and the rest of the Compass kids in making a difference that actually improves your life. Vote with your dollar! Have you ever heard that saying?"

He snickered, realizing that he sounded just like his grandfather, reciting old sayings that very few people knew. But he couldn't help it, it felt quite fitting here.

Ronald continued, impassioned. "You can *always* trust me, Chakra, and the rest of the Compass kids to treat you fairly. We are a club built on honesty, service, and compromise. We invite you to join our ranks, if not today, then go home and come back tomorrow, or next week, or next month. Things only change when we refuse to accept corruption!"

The crowd gave little reaction.

"Well, that discussion went longer than expected, but we were so happy to have you all here! We have to turn the room back over to Mr. Miller now, so we will return to our regular agenda items next week. Thanks everyone for coming!" Chakra stood up and shook a few students' hands while thanking them, trying unsuccessfully to get any of the attendees to sign up for Compass membership, then dismissed the meeting.

Still, she and Ronald were full of hope at the prospect that students were finally seeing the BOTs and GLOs for what they were. They were filled with optimism that they would see the uptick in student enrollments in the Compass Club, proving that students care more about standing up for what is right than going along with a broken system.

It never occurred to them that there wouldn't be enough time for that to happen.

Do Us Part

Sammy walked into the Arco wedding reception hall and was immediately speechless at the beauty all around him. He would expect nothing less than show-stopping style from the effortlessly elegant Reginald, as Sammy had always admired his natural grace.

The cavernous room was a beautiful and ornate celebration of deep plums and creams, with metallic gold accents throughout. These accents reminded Sammy of the sleek golden wedding invitation that had captured his heart when it first arrived at the house. The room had vaulted cathedral ceilings that were nearly three stories high, adding even more drama to the room. Sammy could see the elegant head table up at the front, where Viv's niece Dia and Cleo, both serving as bridesmaids, would sit on either side of the bride and groom.

The wedding at the church had been pleasant enough, though Sammy's mind had a habit of drifting during any church service. Without fail, his attention always landed on the stained-glass windows and their breathtaking mosaics of color and light. He'd sit there wondering who first dreamed up something so strange and perfect, picturing the artisans who pieced them together with impossible precision.

Blame the artist in him, but Sammy was far more interested in figuring out how those windows were made than in deciphering whatever message was being preached beneath them in the church.

Today felt surreal in more ways than one. Sammy had never imagined Reginald getting married. He'd never even seen the man go on a date in all the years he'd known Cleo. The thought had just never come up.

But now, Cleo and Sammy were both forced to see that Reginald had a new and very important job in addition to his role as Cleo's father, and that was to be husband to Genevieve "Viv" Arco.

Wow. Another Arco in the family. That would take some getting used to.

This was also surreal because if you had asked Sammy a month or two ago if he would be socializing with Cleo ever again, he would have been pessimistic about the likelihood of that. Thankfully they had evolved from giving each other the complete silent treatment to now exchanging trite greetings in the hall and cordial interactions during club leadership meetings. But that was hardly socializing. Even standing here now, he wasn't convinced that things would return to anything resembling "normal" today. But as he stood in the same room as her, as an invited guest to such a special event in the story of her life, his heart was full.

"Lleno, we will catch up with you!" His mom and dad had been following close behind Sammy, but now they had trailed off, stopping at the open bar for an evening libation. As parents of a teenager, even sharing a night at a wedding with 150 other strangers still technically counts as date night.

Sammy looked down at his seating card. *Table G, Seats 6-8.* He wondered who they would be sitting with. Secretly he had hoped that he would sit with Cleo, but now seeing the four person head table, he knew that wasn't happening. He imagined the worst-case scenario would probably be sitting with some old church lady fuddy-duddies, boring him with questions about why a boy would ever be wearing a cape, or if he has any "little girlfriends" at school.

Speaking of his fashion, Sammy *dressed* for the event. As in, capital D-R-E-S-S-E-D. He had on a black long-sleeved button up shirt, with a metallic silver vest over it, black pants, his rainbow sneakers (to ensure he didn't look like he was trying too hard), the treasured wristlet, gold and silver nail polish alternating with each nail, and of course…THE CAPE.

He had found a cape in his mother's closet that accompanied one of her formal dresses from years ago, before she had traded in her corporate heels for barn boots. The cape flowed down from his shoulders, reflecting silver and gold iridescent sparkles into the room, like he was his own walking disco ball.

He hated to admit how incredibly hot it was to wear, but unless he wanted to pass out, he would have no choice but to take it off later in the night. At this moment, though, this was his catwalk, and he had no intention of letting a little heat rob him of it.

So, saunter he did.

He reached Table G and saw he was the first one to arrive there. He found seats 6-8 and began to turn over napkins and place their nametags on the plates, claiming the seats. He had to run to the restroom but wanted to ensure his family's places were secure when he got back. After rearranging the seat numbers so he could claim the seats with the best view of the head table, he took the long way to the restroom, working his attention-grabbing stride, and turning heads, the whole way.

When he returned back to the table from the restroom, he noticed that it was full of people now. He saw his parents settling in and putting their napkins on their laps, picking up rolls, and pouring water for everyone. Next to his father he saw what he believed was one of Cleo's single aunts sitting there, and then there were four more people at the table who had their backs to him.

Since he was getting incredibly uncomfortable and boiling hot from his outfit, he figured this was the last time that he would be able to show off his cape at the event. He grabbed the side of the cape and raised it a bit to create a flutter as he arrived at the table, making one more final grand entrance.

Suddenly, his face fell as he saw his other tablemates. His cape's laces, which had been tied in an intentionally ornate bow at Sammy's neck, suddenly came untied and the cape fell to the ground behind him, as if trying to hide itself from the interaction to come. As usual, his face told the full story of what he was feeling.

His mom smiled to overcompensate for Sammy's awkward silence. "Sammy, say hello! Have you met Benjamin's mom and sister? I know you met his dad at the spa the other day…"

He glanced at the other Rosas, all of whom were offering their hands to him to shake, introducing their names one by one.

Wyatt, Didi, Alice. He knew he was never going to remember these.

He noticed that Benjamin's mom looked like she had tears in her eyes. Why did she keep looking up at Reginald? What was upsetting her? Must be shame from having the son that she did. Who could blame her…

He eventually locked eyes with Benjamin, who had a look on his face that was a mix of incredible annoyance, and intense amusement at what he assumed was misery on Sammy's behalf.

Shaking Benjamin's hand was unthinkable. But there was no avoiding it. He had to just get it over with. Rip it off like a band aid.

He offered Benjamin his fingertips, and Benjamin awkwardly shook Sammy's hand as if he was being asked to *kiss* his hand, rather than shake it. Sammy quickly pried his hand out of Benjamin's tight, sweaty grip. He picked up his cape from the floor, draped it over the back of the seat and sat down.

The rest of the dinner was a blur. Sammy tried to disengage as much as he could, but his parents kept peppering him with whispers like "be polite! Talk to them!" or "what is *wrong* with you tonight?"

He spent the entire evening in a daze. He looked over at Benjamin, who was now a permanent trigger reminding him of everything associated with "the arrangement" that was now mentally chasing him every waking minute. While Benjamin was as carefree as a bluebird, Sammy couldn't help but obsessively think about the exact thing he had wanted to avoid thinking about.

In less than two days, Sammy will have broken into a principal's office, forged the clubs' money ledgers to implicate Ronald in a crime he didn't commit, and then watched as the entire school turned on Ronald, leaving his future ruined, with the outcome probably resulting in him getting kicked out of school.

Sammy had spent a lot of time trying to decide which of the three outcomes was upsetting his moral compass the most.

Was he doing it for self-preservation? Perhaps, but at this point, he truly didn't care anymore if he got caught. He was so broken down and battered by his brain's new roommate "Guilt," that he knew that he would probably feel at least some relief to just be caught, face the consequences, and be done with it already. He did know that somewhere deep down, though, he was motivated by trying to save his own hide.

Then, there was the moral reason. Was he doing this for the good of the student body?

No way, he conceded. Sammy knew was making the exact wrong decision for what was best for the rest of the students. They deserved to know what the BOTs and GLOs were doing with the money, with the skewed news, even including what Sammy himself had done. But their rights seemed to be the farthest thing from anyone's priorities right now.

Then, there was Cleo. If he was being honest with himself, Cleo was the primary reason that Sammy had agreed to do this horrible frame-up on Monday. He couldn't bear having someone as sweet and impressionable as her taking the fall for Benjamin and Indigo. It was as if Benjamin was the tiny devil on Sammy's shoulder, and Indigo was the fallen angel on the other, and they both were whispering the same threats and fear into his ears, guiding him in unison to make the bad decision.

As he sat there and watched Benjamin acting out an animated soccer play for the whole table, reveling in the attention without a care in the world, Sammy's internal teapot began to whistle. He knew for Cleo's sake he had to keep it together. The bride and groom's first dance was just about to start, and Sammy knew that if he stayed one more minute in here, he would absolutely explode. "I have to get out of here," he whispered to his mother, grabbed his cape off the back of the chair, and sprinted outside.

He collapsed outside on the steps of the building. His body was twisted up like a pretzel in a subconscious effort to take up as little space as possible — his body language translation for shame. Yet, he was wrapped in his glitter cape, as conspicuous as he could possibly be, visible from a mile away as he shimmered in the light of the moon.

The contrast between these two parts of his subconscious was almost poetic.

Lleno.

As he sat there, cradling his head in his hands and rocking back and forth nervously, he suddenly felt a hand on his shoulder. He couldn't bring himself to look and see who it was. There was truly no one that he wanted to see right now. Benjamin would just want to irritate him, his parents would want to either reprimand or psychoanalyze him, a stranger would want to make banal small talk with him. No, there is simply no one that he would want to speak to in the state he is in. Well, no one except…

"Cleo?" He looked up to see her standing there, dressed in her ridiculous cotton candy bridesmaid dress, which was predictably hideous as all bridesmaid dresses are. Yet both her inner and outer beauty easily overshadowed the absurdness of the gown. All he could see now was the same old Cleo. For one beautiful moment, it was if things had never changed.

Then reality hit him like a ton of bricks again. He slipped back into trite surface level conversations with her, unsure what her intentions were in approaching him.

"Nice party," he said quietly.

"If you say so. Did you meet my *new mommy*?" she said sarcastically in a squeaky baby voice.

They both laughed, desperately needing to let off some steam.

"I did. She's purty," he said in his own attempt at making a toddler voice.

Once she stopped laughing, her face became more serious. "Hey, listen, I'm really sorry that we had to seat you with Benjamin. I knew that was a disaster from the minute it was assigned, but there were truly no other options. I had no idea that my dad invited your family, although I assumed he had probably invited your parents. I figured if you were invited, that you wouldn't come. In a way, I hoped for your sake, that you didn't."

Sammy's heart dropped. "Sorry to disappoint you. I can go…" he began to stand up but tripped on his cape and fell back down.

Cleo giggled, but Sammy was in no mood to laugh.

"Sammy, come on! You think I didn't want you to come? My biggest wish for this trainwreck of a day was that you would show up! It was truly the only thing I was looking forward to this whole day. What I meant was that if you stayed home, you would have been spared sitting with 'Bozomin,'" she said while flashing air quotes.

"How did you know…"

"I hear things. You aren't famous for your subtlety!" She laughed. "But seriously, I'm so happy that you are here. I...I have really missed you."

"Yeah, I'm sorry we kept missing each other tonight, it just seemed like you were always busy doing some wedding stuff..."

"I don't mean that I missed you tonight, I mean that I've missed *you*. For months and months. Like most of the school year, really. I don't know about you, but for me, this has been pure torture. This whole thing has gotten completely out of control."

She sat down next to him on the steps. "I just needed a place to hide because Viv was always at my house. So, I started spending more time at the youth group and things took off from there, I guess. You know, the other week in church, I was listening to my dad talk about friendship, and I finally understood why you were upset that I joined the BOTs. I know what a jerk Benjamin can be and how mean he and the soccer boys can be to you. I'm sorry that my spending time with him hurt you or made you feel like I turned on you. I would never do that on purpose, truly."

Sammy's eyes welled up with tears. He threw his arms around Cleo and squeezed her so tightly that he worried the cheap zipper on the back of her heinous lavender taffeta dress would pop off. He felt butterflies in his stomach, and his heart was reborn, filled again with love.

She continued. "And I'm sorry about the Darla and Megan thing, I'm sorry about the lockers, I'm sorry I filed a complaint with Mr. Miller about you, I'm sorry..."

"Stop! Pull yourself together, have some dignity, girl!" Sammy sassed to lighten the mood.

He paused, rewinding her apology in his mind. "Wait, *you* were the one who reported me to Mr. Miller?"

"Yeah, I was really angry that day and I wanted to get back at you, I don't know…if I could take it back I would. In a heartbeat. I love you."

"Thanks, Cleo. I love you too. And I'm so sorry too, for not being here for all the hard times and adjustments you've been going through with Viv and your dad. This must have been so tough to accept having a new woman come into your life. Are you okay?" He looked in her eyes with sincere concern.

"Yes, I'll be okay. Although I really needed your hilarious commentary when the dress options were first presented. I could hear your voice in my head… 'hmm should you pick the one that looks like a bunch of purple grapes, or the one like purple cotton candy?'" She laughed.

Sammy started laughing too. "That is *exactly* the word I used for this dress. In my head of course. Cotton candy. Yeesh." They shared a smile.

"Hey, by the way, Sammy," Cleo lowered her voice to a whisper. "Please don't frame Ronald on my account. Even though I helped with the Prism bribes for Benjamin, I knew what I was doing. I should have been brave enough to tell him no. I will take the consequences for my actions. You are totally innocent in all of this, and so is Ronald."

"I'm *definitely* not innocent, and let's leave it at that. Besides, we can't have you getting kicked out of school! The minister's daughter being suspended for stealing money? Ronald will be fine. He is super smart, and his grades will outweigh any disciplinary issues when he goes to apply to college. And hey, I told him he should have picked a side!" he said with a forced chuckle, but nothing about this felt funny to him. He simply wanted to alleviate Cleo's guilt with some levity.

"You really think so?" she said with deep concern in her eyes.

"Everything will be just fine. You can trust me, Cleo. I'll always be there for you." He opened his cape, and Cleo snuggled her body under it as he wrapped it around her bare shoulders to keep her warm.

For the first time in nearly a year, it felt as if things were falling into place. There was just one more thing Sammy had to do.

THE BLAME GAME

Sammy couldn't sleep at all last night. Sundays are usually hard for him anyway, as his mind always raced in anticipation and dread as the return to school on Monday looms large. But this Monday was different. The entire morning, he hadn't heard one word that his teachers had said. He hoped he wouldn't be quizzed on any of it. He could probably get Cleo's notes if he needed them.

Ah, it was good to have her back.

As the bell announcing the start of lunch rang, Sammy closed his locker and headed towards the school office. His palms were sweating, his legs were shaking, and his stride was hesitant, as if he was trying to slow the situation down both literally and figuratively.

He coached himself along. Almost there. In ten minutes, this will all be over.

He turned the final corner as he neared Principal Goldblum's office. Suddenly, he saw her in the hallway, coming at him. She was wearing her outdoor jacket and carrying her purse, walking away from her office with her keys in her hand.

"Hey Sammy!" She smiled at him. "Have a nice lunch!"

You too. A nice LONG lunch.

"Thanks Principal G! You too." He smiled an innocent smile as he passed by her, wiping his sopping wet palms on his pants as he walked. He reached her office and looked both ways before opening the door to ensure the hallway was clear.

It was.

As he entered the unlocked door, he saw that Kwame's desk was uncharacteristically empty. To anyone else, his desk being empty plus an unlocked door would have seemed to be a huge mistake. But Sammy knew this was no error.

He looked up at the camera that normally had an annoying flashing red light on it, but today, it was dark. The coast was clear. He dashed into Principal Goldblum's office and closed the door behind him.

He fumbled with the various loose sheets of paper and Post-It notes that he was carrying in his pockets, given to him by Indigo, Benjamin, and Cleo. This included combinations to lock boxes, tips about what days to edit the ledger, what notes to put down on each day, etc.

Sammy succeeded in opening all the lock boxes and organizing the specific pens that he had been given by the others to match the original pens used. Red, blue, black, felt tip, ball point, he was prepared for anything. He laid everything out neatly and prepared to make the changes. He unfolded the main instruction sheet, typed neatly by Indigo with hand scribbles in the margins by Benjamin.

1. Edit the withdrawals on the GLO and BOT ledgers. For any reference to Cleo, Benjamin, or Indigo making withdrawals, erase their names altogether for some, and keep their names for others, but misspell them and make errors that will raise red flags that the withdrawals are fraudulent. This will make it seem as if Ronald made these errors as part of his cover-up.

2. Indicate a deposit on the Compass ledger for the exact combined amount taken from the BOTs and GLOs accounts. Attribute it to Ronald.

3. Make note of a later personal cash withdrawal by Ronald from the Compass ledger for the same amount of money that he "stole"

from the GLOs and BOTs to explain why the funds aren't in his account.

As Sammy stood there, looking down at the ledgers, he saw the withdrawal for the money he himself had stolen to satisfy the Bruce bribe. Sammy marked it down as "shelter cleaning supplies." He knew that it would never be flagged, and he would never get caught unless Bruce blabbed.

His justification for doing this whole frame-up as some necessary evil to save himself didn't make any sense now. He wasn't at significant risk of being exposed. For all intents and purposes, he was in the clear at this moment. He began to lose his courage, reconsidering the whole thing.

Then he remembered something else. Cleo *was* at risk, though, because it was only a matter of time until students caught on to the newspaper scheme. Once they figured that out, they would approach the Prism for explanations, and ultimately it wouldn't be long until it was uncovered that Cleo gave bribes to convince the reporters to risk their jobs.

Sammy felt a renewed sense of purpose that he must edit these ledgers to protect his friend.

He hesitantly picked up a pen, and began making the necessary changes diligently, ensuring that Cleo was protected. He switched pens, and matched handwritings the best that he could, and did his best to cover her tracks. Then he stood up, confident that the paper trail tying her to stealing the money was now gone.

Sammy reorganized each lock box in an orderly fashion, put the edited ledgers in each of them, and closed two of them up leaving the third open (as part of the plan), and entered in the passcodes one last time to secure the contents.

But Sammy had deviated from the plan in one important way. He always marched to the beat of his own drummer, and this was no exception. He just hoped Cleo would forgive him.

He stood there, proud of himself for the first time in months. His job was done. He snuck out of the office and ran to the lunchroom, only a few minutes late. Hopefully no one noticed.

The rest of the day, Sammy was a nervous wreck. He had passed Benjamin and Indigo separately today, Indigo in the hallway and Benjamin in the lunchroom, each of them attempting to solicit a thumbs up from him to confirm that the deed had been done.

He knew that the truth would come out soon, because Kwame's final job was to alert Principal Goldblum that one of the lock boxes had been left open, which was supposed to be suspicious to him because no one had signed in to the office to gain permission to access them. This was meant to launch a full investigation by her, where she would find "Ronald's" ledger tampering, and consequences would rain down on him, shielding the others from exposure of bribery or Prism news manipulations.

This is what was *supposed* to happen.

Now, the only thing there was to do was wait.

UNTOUCHABLE

"Hey! What are you doing?" Sitting in his classroom and spacing out at the end of the day, Sammy suddenly heard raised voices outside in the hallway.

He'd recognize that voice anywhere.

Ronald.

"Sure, I'll come down to the office to speak with you, but I can assure you, I didn't do anything!" Sammy rushed to the door to see Ronald walking past his classroom with Principal Goldblum on one side, and the EHS security guard on his other side, holding on to Ronald's elbow as he escorted him down the hall.

Sammy turned as white as a sheet.

What was going on? This didn't make sense! He frantically looked around the classroom, noticing that everyone was looking out the door curiously. Whispers had already begun that Ronald must have stolen something or cheated from someone. The EHS grapevine was already in full effect, twisting and contorting rumors with each student that it passed through.

Sammy then saw Cleo looking at him, her eyes full of regret and shame. He continued to look desperately around the room, looking for answers where there were none. He stepped out of the classroom to see Ronald and his guides just as they turned the corner towards Principal Goldblum's office and disappeared from sight. Sammy saw

Indigo's head pop into the hallway from her upper-school classroom, watching the same spectacle.

"Psst!" Indigo turned to see Sammy motioning for her to come to him. He crossed the hall and huddled in the closed doorway of Mr. Miller's workshop. "Indigo, what is going on? Why is Ronald getting into trouble?"

She looked at him with a confused look on her face. "What do you mean? You changed the ledgers to implicate him. Things are going exactly to plan."

Sammy shook his head. "No, but I didn't."

"Didn't what?" Indigo asked knowingly.

"I…I didn't put down Ronald's name. I put down mine. I left him and the Compass Club out of this." He started talking very quickly, trying to get his entire justification out before she cut him off.

Sammy continued. "Look, there was no reason that he should be blamed. It's true that I didn't offer the bribes to Darla or Megan, but I am *definitely* not innocent. Between Ronald, Cleo, and I, there is no doubt that I deserve to be punished the most. Now you and Benjamin, on the other hand, that is a different story…" he said as he shot her a judgmental glare. "But I don't understand, why am I not the one in her office?"

Indigo stood silently, looking down the hallway that had been empty for a while now.

"Indy! What is going on?" Sammy implored.

"Look, it's taken care of. Just leave it alone." She started to walk into her classroom.

"INDIGO!" Sammy's voice projected much louder than he anticipated it would. She rushed back out to stop him from causing a scene. He brought his voice back to a whisper. "What did you do?"

"I told you, Sammy, I will *never* let anything happen to my GLO Club. No one will get in my way. The mission is too important." Her face was intense.

"What are you saying?" Sammy asked.

"Come on, Pepper, did you really think that we wouldn't find out what you did? Kwame went and checked that everything was in order, and when he saw what you did, he told Benjamin and I everything. He saw your name on the ledgers for all the withdrawals and bribes, and he saw you left the Compass ledger untouched. It was a sloppy attempt too, because you had times and days that you were in class or on the road at soccer meets. No one would have believed you anyway. But even if they did, we can't have *you* being blamed, because *we* can't be blamed. Don't you get it?"

Sammy was in shock. "So, what did you do?"

"Benjamin and I went back and changed the ledgers to say what we needed them to say. It's all done. Ronald, and the Compass Club, are both history. He's going down." She was shockingly aloof.

"But I was willing to take the blame! Why couldn't you let me? I wouldn't have said a word."

"Sammy, our clubs are too important to fail. No one needs Ronald *or* the Compass Club. But the GLOs, and the BOTs, we are *important*. We do good work, we have lots of financial support from the students, and we can make things happen around here. We can't risk having one of our clubs close up, otherwise there is no reason for the other club either, and then we *both* go down. Benjamin and I are in complete agreement on this. For once!" She laughed to try to lighten the mood, but Sammy was having none of it.

"So, that's it? The BOTs are our enemies, except when we need to unite to kill the competition?"

Indigo nodded distantly. "Yes Sammy, that's *it*."

"Don't you think that the kids are going to figure out soon about the newspapers? I mean, all it will take is for one student to talk to a friend from the other club, and they will find out that they are reading different news. Then what? Mr. Miller will shut the whole thing down!" Sammy proudly pointed out this flaw in their plan.

Indigo smiled condescendingly. "Sammy don't be naïve. Mr. Miller knows all about it. Do you really think that the faculty advisor for the Prism, not to mention the entire journalism program, doesn't know that his reporters have created two different versions of the paper?

Sammy's face fell in disbelief.

She continued. "Darla and Megan said that when the first differing news issues were released, Mr. Miller confronted them about it. They had no choice but to admit their part in the dual news scheme. They assumed that he would take disciplinary action against them, but instead, Mr. Miller told them that he was willing to turn his head, as long as the newspapers continue to fly off the shelves and be as popular as they are. Apparently, the journalism program was in jeopardy before all of this, but because the popularity of these different papers is so high, he is willing to do whatever it takes to keep the paper in business and the journalism program in the curriculum."

Sammy was emphatic. "That's not possible! He told me that he would never compromise his journalistic ethics. He said that having trustworthy news is the most important thing for a school or a country, and we will lose our freedoms if the leaders of the news ever compromise on this!"

"Well, I guess keeping his job and selling papers was more important."

Sammy stood there silently as Indigo twisted her feathers. He had looked up to Mr. Miller so much, and to find out that he, as the head of the entire news outlet was part of this corruption…Sammy was devastated to watch a hero fall. He had never really looked up to a teacher before. And look what it got him.

Sammy now considered himself out of the hero game.

Indigo saw the rush of emotions on his face. "Look, I'm sorry that things didn't turn out the way you planned. But…" her voice became full of comforting pep, "you are a GLO leader, and we will always have your back! You can *always* count on me!" She smiled, forced a hug on him, and rushed back into her class.

Sammy stood there in the hallway; his body frozen in shock. He looked into his classroom to see Cleo looking out at him, with a furrowed brow.

Did she know what was going on? Was she a part of this, or living completely in the dark like he was? Could she have betrayed Sammy after they just made up?

He had to find out. Now.

He motioned for her to come to him. She grabbed the girls' bathroom key from the classroom hook and nervously snuck out into the hallway, looking concerned. "Is everything okay?"

"Did you see Ronald just get taken away? It was horrible," Sammy said, visibly emotional.

"I know, it is terrible. Even though I feel horrible about it, I really wanted to thank you for trying to protect me. But..." she paused, looking sick to her stomach. "I need to tell the truth. I can't live with myself. I am going to go to Principal Goldblum and tell her that it was me, not Ronald, that took the money."

Sammy was so proud of her. For being true to herself. For being brave. For choosing honor in the end. But even her devoted will to do the right thing couldn't stop the out-of-control snowball that was rushing down the hill, threatening all in its tracks.

"You won't be able to do that, Cleo. Benjamin won't let you." Sammy had a defeated look in his eye.

"Won't *let* me? What do you mean? How do you know?" Cleo asked inquisitively.

Realizing that they both were trapped, their freedoms stripped from them like animals on a factory farm, he responded. "Trust me, I just know. You must leave it alone now."

Mrs. Adams popped her head out of the classroom. "What's going on out here? Get back in here, both of you!" Cleo, looking back at

Sammy confused, nervously retreated back into the classroom while he stared down the hallway, hoping in vain to see Ronald round the corner, free from his fate.

Sadly, that was not to be.

Sammy felt entombed in this scheme. He felt that his choices had been taken away, and that he could neither escape the system, nor actively participate in it in good conscience.

He stewed in his anger. This is what you get when you let childish games run amok! If adults had been involved in creating clubs like this, we never would have seen the selfishness or corruption that happened here.

He paused, considering an even scarier alternative. *Or would we?*

Acknowledgments and Reflection

If you made it all the way to this page, thank you. Truly.

You just spent hours inside a world that, in many ways, reflects our own. A world where people mean well but still hurt each other.

Where love and loyalty sometimes collide.

And where even the best intentions can get tangled up in the messy business of being human.

I personally know people like all of these characters. I'm guessing you do too. They're all wonderful, and they're all flawed. I love them for both of those reasons.

I wrote *The New We* because I was tired of watching people forget how to listen, or worse, refuse to.

I wanted to explore what happens when caring turns into choosing sides, and how friendship can still survive when the world keeps trying to split it apart.

I wanted to remind myself (and maybe you, too) that empathy is not weakness, and compassion isn't compromise.

They're both forms of strength — the kind that keeps us human when everything around us is shouting to pick a team.

To every reader who's ever felt caught in the middle, unsure which "side" they're supposed to be on:

You are not alone.

You don't have to choose between your heart and your hope for the world. You can believe passionately, love deeply, and still reach across the line. In fact, that's where real courage begins.

To everyone who helped bring this story to life — thank you.

To my husband + soulmate — thank you for being the strongest person I will ever know, wrapped up and packaged as the kindest and sweetest human being I will ever meet.

To my son + twin flame — thank you for being my inspiration for this book and every other element in my life.

To my brother — thank you for being the best friend that an angsty 90s girl could ask for.

To my parents — thank you for your love and inspiration through the years.

To my extended family and friends — thank you for supporting me throughout my life, and I hope you enjoy the Easter eggs hidden throughout this book from our lives together.

To the readers, teachers, and young dreamers who see yourselves in these pages — thank you for proving that stories still matter, and minds can still stay open to consider and discuss tough topics.

And to all the people in my own life who remind me every day that kindness is a superpower: you know who you are, and I couldn't do any of this without you.

If there's one thing I hope you take from this book, it's this:

People aren't puzzles to solve or battles to win.

They're stories to be heard.

And when we take the time to really listen — to understand, not just to respond — we start building the kind of world we all want to live in. Here's to friendship, to conversation, to second chances.

Here's to the brave and beautiful mess of being human — together.

I consider all of you part of my *New We*.

Stacy McKay

About the Author

STACY MCKAY is an award-winning entrepreneur, international educator, and author with over twenty-five years of experience working at the intersection of culture, identity, and belonging. Her career has spanned international education, university administration, immigration law, organizational leadership, and the founding of an international organization that helped thousands of students find their place in the world through study abroad.

Originally from rural Pennsylvania, she now writes from coastal Florida, where she lives with her husband John, their son Leo, and her impish Persian cat Noelle, who regularly interrupts her work (and is probably snoozing on Stacy's keyboard right now). Another love of her life is the em dash, and she will not abandon it simply for fear of being perceived as an AI bot!

The release of *The New We* continues her lifelong mission to inspire empathy, curiosity, and understanding in young people.

WWW.STACYMCKAY.COM